# THE

# ANGEL

# EFFECT

# THE
# ANGEL
# EFFECT

## WE ARE NEVER ALONE

## JOHN GEIGER

HarperCollins*Publishers*Ltd

Published by HarperCollins Publishers Ltd.

First Canadian edition

The names of some individuals appearing in this book have been changed,
at their request, to protect their privacy.

HarperCollins books may be purchased for educational, business, or
sales promotional use through our Special Markets Department.

HarperCollins Publishers Ltd
2 Bloor Street East, 20th Floor
Toronto, Ontario, Canada
M4W 1A8

*www.harpercollins.ca*

Library and Archives Canada Cataloguing in Publication information is available.

ISBN 978-1-44341-359-6

Editorial production by *Marra*thon Production Services. www.marrathon.net

BOOK DESIGN BY JANE RAESE
Text set in 12-point Fairfield Medium

Printed and bound in Canada
WC 9 8 7 6 5 4 3 2 1

FOR MARINA

# CONTENTS

# CONTENTS

# JAMES

In 2008 I experienced something extraordinary at a moment of great pain, something that has altered the way I think about the world and has given me firsthand insight into a profound mystery.

It happened to me when I had nearly completed writing *The Third Man Factor: Surviving the Impossible,* and it brought the phenomenon of what scientists call the sensed presence vividly to life for me. That book arose from my growing realization—gleaned from my own experiences in the Arctic, my conversations with explorers and field scientists, and reading the published accounts of explorers—that people under enormous stress, sometimes at the edge of death, often experience a sense of an incorporeal being beside them who encourages them to survive. Climbers refer to it as the "third man."

I assembled a trove of such stories and investigated religious, psychological, and neurological explanations for the phenomenon. In the process I also published a scholarly study, "The Sensed Presence as a Coping Resource in Extreme Environments," with Professor Peter Suedfeld, a renowned expert of the psychological effects of exploration who has also advised NASA.

Suedfeld and I identified four indisputable facts about the sensed presence, notably that they occur to otherwise mentally normal, physically healthy individuals; they arise in stressful situations; they serve as a coping resource in that they aid the individual's efforts to survive; and that, despite various theories, their source remains a mystery.[1]

The sensed presence is far greater than the simple feeling that we all sometimes have when, alone at night or when walking down an alley, we feel that someone is there. Various reductive explanations have been offered, and although many of those indeed may play some role, none of them comes anywhere near to capturing the richness and profundity of the experience, which person after person describes as among the most important of their lives. Peter Suedfeld and I argued for the need to better understand the "dramatic helpfulness of the sensed presence, which includes not only encouragement, but also factual information ... and, on occasion, physical intervention."

That study, and *The Third Man Factor,* held closely to the view that you had to be astride Everest or engaged in an equally harrowing pursuit, such as those undertaken by solo sailors, polar explorers, and astronauts, to experience the phenomenon. It worked wonderfully as a way to introduce the radical idea. But in fact, it is not the case that explorers and adventurers are the sole recipients of such interventions. Far from it.

I opened *The Third Man Factor* with the experience of Ron DiFrancesco, the last person to escape the South Tower of the World Trade Center on 9/11, who told me that he survived that day because an angel helped him. DiFrancesco was just going about his routine business when terror struck. He found himself trapped in a smoke-filled stairwell, above the point of impact of United Airlines Flight 175, with flames and a collapsed wall obstructing his escape. Other people were with him on a landing, some apparently unconscious, when, he says, an angel urged him to carry on. It addressed him by his first name and gave him encouragement, telling him, "Hey! You can do this."

DiFrancesco felt that he was literally helped to his feet and then guided on, saying, "It led me to the stairwell, led me to break through, led me to run through the fire. ... There was obviously somebody encouraging me: 'That's not where you go, you don't go toward the fire.'"[2] He covered his head with his arms and literally fought through it. He believes the flames continued for three stories. Only after he got safely through the debris, to below the flames, did he sense the angel leave. It had been with him for five minutes. When talking to him, I was struck by the idea that something extraordinary can touch everyday people caught up in crisis situations they weren't looking for or were in anyway prepared for.

Then, following the publication of that book, hundreds of people began to step forward with their stories, accounts that do not involve high-altitude climbs—though I do still get plenty of those. Intriguingly, however, these stories often include quite routine stresses, the sorts of hardships that we all potentially face in our lives when confronted by grief, physical and sexual assaults, automobile accidents, raging fires, and bank heists as well as a result of long illnesses, the pain of childbirth, the despair of alcoholism, and even in cases of persistent loneliness.

Others sent me testimonials handed down from loved ones who had served in war or survived other personal calamities. They wrote to me from Australia, the UK, Spain, the United States, and Israel, and they were men, women, teenagers, and seniors. Some of my friends and acquaintances also came forward to say it had happened to them. These stories are every bit as compelling as those of the explorers and adventurers. This phenomenon is universal; it can happen to any one of us.

And then it happened to me.

JAMES ENTERED OUR LIVES AT 1:26 A.M. on Friday, June 15, 2007, three minutes after his brother Sebastian. Despite a diagnosis of hypoplastic left heart syndrome, a rare congenital heart condition first detected in an ultrasound, he declared himself a strong little boy, very much a fighter. He was fine when inside my wife, Marina, and indeed he had thrived, surprising us by coming in at four pounds, nine ounces—two ounces heavier than his older brother.

He was a gorgeous baby. He looked normal; in fact, he was normal in every other way, but basically James had half of a heart, as his left ventricle was severely underdeveloped. From the moment of his birth the clock started ticking.

We had been trying to have a second child for five years. After our first was born, Marina's obstetrician said that if we wanted another, we should not delay, that time was not our friend. But the demands of new parenthood overwhelmed us so much that we set aside the thought of immediately having another child.

By the time we were ready, the ground rules had changed, and we needed fertility treatments. Finally, after much effort, we produced a pregnancy—twin boys. This was joyous news, but the very serious diagnosis that an ultrasound delivered after twenty weeks soon tempered our happiness.

Among the options presented to us was the selective "termination" of the second fetus, a procedure that would also have had a slight risk of jeopardizing the healthy child. Even without the risk to the other twin, it was an unacceptable option for us both. We opted to see the pregnancy through, bracing for the trauma that lay ahead. We read everything we could find about the condition. We met with a couple who had a child with hypoplastic left heart syndrome and whose son was doing quite well given the severity of the medical journey he was on. The boy was in school. Looking at him you wouldn't know, they said. But we also understood that his was an exceptional case.

The twins were born prematurely, and this further complicated James's condition. At his birth, James cried briefly, the only noise I ever heard him make. He was literally rushed from the delivery room—each was. The two boys were then immediately placed in separate incubators. I was unable to photograph them together. Shortly after their birth James was whisked away to the Critical Care Unit at the Hospital for Sick Children in Toronto. Sebastian remained across the street in the Intensive Care Unit of Mount Sinai Hospital. Marina was also hospitalized for several days.

After James was born he developed some symptoms of respiratory distress and later was treated for necrotizing entercolitis. He stabilized twenty-four hours after birth and was maintained on mechanical ventilation and other support—in the words of his critical care physician, written with clipped detachment on his chart—"while his parents worked through their concern regarding James' long term prognosis."[3]

We were presented with two horrible options: one was to have open-heart surgery on a premature baby with a serious risk of brain damage, to be followed by two more open-heart surgeries before the age of three. These would attempt to construct a heart that could sustain James through his child-hood. Needless to say there was a high risk of death at every turn. Sudden death between surgeries was also a possibility. Then, by about age twenty, James would require a heart transplant, as his surgically constructed heart would begin to give out. This was the upside option.

The other choice was simply to remove life support and allow James to die as children with this condition had always done before the heroic measures of modern medicine.

Despite the vast experience of the specialists at the hospital, their policy was to offer no advice whatsoever. In hospital jargon it's called "Patient Autonomy." Their policy was to leave the decision entirely to the parents, regardless of whether they were equipped to make it. It was a cop-out really, possibly designed to protect the hospital's interests ahead of our own. It is presented as a patient's right, the right to make decisions about medical care without health care providers influencing the decision. They are allowed only to "educate" patients or, in our case, the parents of an infant patient, in an either-or sort of way. There is a great deal of debate among medical ethicists and practitioners as to whether this is the correct approach, especially as some studies show that "many patients do not have a strong preference for autonomy ... and many even prefer a paternalistic model."[4]

The hospital record the critical care physician wrote put it much more starkly than it seemed at the time, with a young life hanging in the balance: "I and others met with them several times over this period to give them information regarding the options for palliative surgery. The increased potential for an adverse neurologic outcome in general and specific to James' prematurity were discussed at length."[5] In fact, we were presented with a monstrous situation that no parent should ever have to face and decisions that no parent should ever have to make, especially as it concerned a life just born and so full of promise.

It was an agonizing trial. With Marina still hospitalized and Sebastian in the ICU, I crossed University Avenue countless times each day going from one hospital to the other. We had the joy of one healthy, though premature, baby to celebrate, and we also had a slow-motion emergency unfolding across the street. I spent hours sitting with James. He was constantly monitored. I rubbed his feet. He briefly opened his eyes during the first couple of days of his life. I spoke to him. I told him that his daddy was there and that I loved him. I felt every minute was precious. His nurse, a wonderful, heroic young woman, gave me a card from James, with tiny handprints, for Father's Day.

We were under unimaginable stress. Marina was recovering alone in the hospital. Grabbing a few hours sleep at home one night, I experienced an episode of bioscopic feedback, in which the events of the previous days were replayed at high speed. We consulted a minister, a social worker, a psychologist—none of it seemed to help. Some of our friends and family were supportive, and my stepmum, Jean, flew in from Calgary to help. Others apparently despaired over what they could do or say, so they said and did little. Many did no doubt pray for James, as did we. Marina was recovering, and she and I visited James together, as did our oldest son, Alvaro. We had plaster casts made of James's hands and feet. Very quickly the situation worsened, and ultimately the decision was taken away from us. I feel I bear some of the responsibility for this, for the delay in our attempts to understand what to do didn't help his chances, if there were any chances. To this day I don't really know.

James was slipping away, as were our dreams for him.

On his last day I asked the attending physician if we could take James outside, just for a few minutes, but I was told that was impossible. I wanted him to experience the warmth of the sun, to hear some birds, to feel a breeze. Instead, he was wheeled from the Critical Care Unit to another room just down the hall. According to the hospital record, "James was extubated while in his parents arms and he died approximately one hour thereafter." How can I describe that hour? A horror unlike any other, certainly. One without any of the consolations that accompany many deaths, such as thoughts about the well-lived long life. There are no happy memories to hold on to.

The hour was spent in a room specially designed for a child's death, with the sort of chairs, books on grief, hand-knitted throws, stuffed toys, and other accoutrements that psychologists no doubt believe make the experience more comfortable, bearable, or survivable. I shudder to think of the pain and grief that has been suffered in that room over time. At least we got to hold James finally. Our baby died at 11:11 P.M. on Thursday, June 21.

Marina is a woman of faith, and she derived strength from that. Hard as it was on her—and it was terribly hard—the idea that James was somehow in a better place consoled her. I admire her for that. I have never had such certainty or conviction, and in fact this experience left me feeling bereft or abandoned by faith, so I coped in other ways. I felt James had been denied the only chance he had at life. I was then—and, to a certain extent, remain today—angry about the situation, the injustice of his short life, and his death. As far as I was concerned, our prayers had not been answered. A few days after that, on a sweltering June afternoon, we gathered around a tiny plot in a Toronto cemetery. We had a few words from Kenneth Grahame's *The Wind in the Willows* carved into James's gravestone. They come from a chapter titled, "The Piper at the Gates of Dawn": "Row on, Mole, row! For the music and the call must be for us."

Here's what I said at James's internment:

"We cannot but help ask ourselves: Why this boy?

"We seek the comfort of our faith. But still we ask ourselves: Lord, why this little boy?

"What could this innocent life have done to have earned such a fate: to have received the gift of life and then have had it snatched back so soon and, frankly, so cruelly?

"And we think of the things that we can now never know: What would James Geiger have made of his life? What kind of journeys would he have undertaken? How would he have loved, how would he have lived, had he been given that chance?

"There are no answers to these questions. Only a terrible void, a pain that we will carry all of the rest of our lives. That, along with the memory of a beautiful little boy dying in our arms."

In our grief we then set out to try to mend our terribly damaged family and to focus our attention on our two beautiful, healthy, surviving sons.

The days passed, and then the weeks. I buried myself in my work, hoping that when I finally put my head up again the pain would be gone, but it wasn't. I must have been more brittle than I had supposed.

One evening I was up late in my study working as the rest of the household slept. I remember taking a break and walking upstairs to the rooftop deck. A wind had come up in advance of a thunderstorm. I sat for a few minutes on a lounge chair, at once sad and exhilarated by the fresh and cool air. I then went back down to my computer and resumed writing. My old border collie, Kirby, sauntered in and laid down by my feet.

Maybe an hour after that, I had a powerful sense that someone was watching me, literally standing close behind my right shoulder. I felt I could see someone in my peripheral vision. It was not eerie or unsettling in any way because I knew who it was. I surprised myself by saying aloud, "James?" But I didn't need to turn and look. It was a powerful, vivid awareness. Kirby looked up. James was not as he had been seared into my memory: an infant lying connected to tubes and monitors, a pair of cardboard "sunglasses" to protect his closed eyes from the bright hospital lights. He impressed me now as full grown, or at least I had the sense that he was at the height of an older child or adult. Finally, I turned fully, expecting to see him. I saw nothing, yet I knew he was there.

It did not last long, perhaps only a few minutes. There was no communication as such. But it was powerful, and to this day it remains in my mind something profound. It was as though I had a glimpse into a different world of possibilities—for James and for me. I didn't feel surprised or sad, nor did I experience a longing for what might have been. Instead, I had a feeling as though a love greater than any other had embraced me. I felt better for the encounter, almost like I knew him—a child I could not possibly have known. And somehow I was more at peace than I had been for a long time. It was him, but it was greater than him.

This was very emotional and also very personal. I wanted to include something in the book I was writing at the time, but the experience felt too raw, and to share it was simply not something I could bring myself to do, even with those very close to me. It wasn't that I was concerned about what they would think—that didn't matter to me. But I did feel like it was something intimate, something I needed to protect. I also wondered whether the fact I was writing a book about the third man, about sensed-presence experiences, might have contributed to what happened to me in some way. Was it only the power of suggestion? To be honest, I didn't know what to do with it, so I put it, along with James's few possessions, including his blanket, in a little box that we keep in my office. Marina suggested I dedicate *The Third Man Factor* to James, which I did, and left it at that.

It was only after that book was published and hundreds of other people stepped forward with their own stories and shared with me deeply personal experiences—and doubtless also after the healing that comes with the passage of time—did I feel I could open up that little box.

I began to look at the phenomenon with fresh eyes. After all, it had not happened to me on a mountaintop or in the barrens of Arctic Canada but in my own home. I had so many questions. To begin with: Why me? I was not in mortal danger when it happened, certainly in emotional distress, but nothing of the scale of climbers clinging to life in the Death Zone of Everest. And why then? It had not happened during the worst of the trauma, in the days leading up to or at the time of James's death. It happened later, though I was still grappling with what I—we—had been through.

And finally I opened the box because I wanted to understand the fundamental mystery: Was it a religious experience? Does James exist in an afterlife? Or was this some process of my brain to help me cope with what I have been through? This book is my journey of understanding.

DADDY, CAN YOU SWALLOW ANGELS
WHEN THEY FALL DOWN FROM THE SKY?

—*Sebastian Geiger, age four*

# -1-

# THE

# TUCSON

# NUN

## THE SENSED-PRESENCE PHENOMENON

IT WAS A SUNDAY AFTERNOON IN MARCH IN ARIZONA, and the hot Tucson sun beat down on a brilliant yellow sports car. Jane Pottle had just driven her husband to work and now was passing down a broad boulevard on her way home. In an instant she was unconscious. She saw swirling stars and went limp. She had no idea, quite literally, what hit her. Later, she learned that a large Cadillac, driven by an eighty-year-old man, had shot out from a side street on the right, with trees obscuring its movement until the last moment. It smashed into her sports car, throwing it back twenty feet and virtually destroying its front end.

Jane had a vivid sense of fighting to come to. It took several minutes for her to regain some awareness of her surroundings, but even then she could not focus her vision except on the bright sunshine that poured into the shattered automobile. Her head had cracked the windshield, her forehead had split open, and blood was pouring from the injury. Her chest had hit the steering wheel, but at the time she had no idea what was happening to her. "I remember thinking, 'Why is it hard to breathe? Why can't I move?' I then realized I was gravely hurt (was I in an accident?) but I was too weak to help myself. I started to panic, thinking I was going to die."[1]

Jane prayed for help. Her breathing became more and more rapid and more labored. She knew she was in great danger. "That is when I suddenly felt a warm, soft hand holding mine," she said. "I was not startled; I was happy and relieved that someone was there. I could not see her, but thought, 'Gee, someone has sat in the passenger seat to help me! Maybe a passerby.'"

Her eyes could not focus on the person, but she knew it was a woman and could feel her hand and hear her calm, soothing voice. It seemed almost like a whisper in her ear and, indeed, inside her head. While the soft hands clasped on to hers, the woman's voice spoke with extreme clarity: "Calm down. Breathe very slowly. Help is on the way." It was more than simple advice—it was a command. The voice repeated, "Calm down. Breathe very slowly," until Jane cast off her panic and practiced breathing slowly as the voice advised. "I had the feeling I only had minutes to live. I assumed she was a real, tangible person in authority who knew exactly what to do. Yes, I feel the woman was there to ensure my survival. I would have died without her help."

Jane gradually became aware of many voices around the car, but she could not understand what they were saying. She just practiced breathing extremely slowly as the woman suggested. The woman—Jane thought she was a nun—assured her that she had no reason to panic and told Jane that she would not leave her side. Jane felt relieved and decided to just concentrate on surviving. The accident occurred just around the corner from a hospital, directly in front of a church. She had no concept of how much time passed, though it seemed like a good while before paramedics arrived. Her legs were pinned in the wreckage, so firefighters had to pry open the door to free her, which took another ten minutes. When they succeeded, Jane realized her helper had left. "The nun's hand had disappeared at the same time the paramedics grabbed me," she remembered. "I just assumed she made way for them. She was there right up to the last second. It had seemed to me that she dissipated. But I thought she was there just to keep me company until help arrived. I didn't think it strange that she left; I did, however, think it strange at the time that she seemed to have just disappeared into thin air and none of the other paramedics were speaking to her as they entered the car. But I had other things on my mind, so I didn't dwell on it."

The paramedics worked quickly to assess her condition. They gave her an injection and asked her whom they should contact. She said her husband's phone number was in her purse. She was lifted onto a gurney and then into an ambulance before being conveyed to the hospital. The paramedics were talking loudly to her all the way, ensuring that she did not slip into unconsciousness, and Jane was now more alert and coherent.

The last thing she remembered before entering surgery was the sound of the gurney going clickety-clack as the medical personnel hurried it down the hospital hallways. Her surgery lasted five hours, from three o'clock to eight in the evening. She was clinically dead for two minutes at 7:30 P.M. Soon she lapsed into a coma and remained in that state for a month, hooked up to life support.

Jane had some level of awareness during the coma. She noticed the nurses' shift changes and registered when doctors made their rounds. She also felt as if a woman visited her each day during this period and put a red rose on her night table. She could smell the strong, sweet fragrance of the single rose as the aroma filled the room. To this day red roses are her favorite flower. Later, when she emerged from the coma, she asked the nurses about the visitor, and they insisted there was no woman visitor. No one other than her husband and parents were allowed to see her in the intensive care unit.

She also asked about the woman in her car, the woman whom she feels saved her life. The nurses tracked down the head paramedic at the accident scene, who assured her no one else was in the car when they arrived and confirmed that, in fact, no one would have been able to enter the car through either door.

The small vehicle had crumpled like an accordion in the collision. In took the jaws of life to open the driver-side door to get her out. Jane had no memory of the equipment or the noise it made to retrieve her. "I guess I tuned it all out and focused on breathing. If I had continued to panic during that time, I would have died. My ribs were broken and had punctured a lung, which was bleeding. My nose was ripped off (but still attached and hanging to the side), and my insides were slowly filling with blood. Indeed, if I had continued to panic, the blood would have filled my lungs and airways, and I would have drowned."

It was a long and difficult recovery. Even after she emerged from the coma Jane had to learn how to breathe properly, eat, and walk again. Both her arms and legs remained in traction for three months. After she was released from the hospital, she remained on crutches for another six months. "The doctors say it was a miracle that I survived. I was told by the doctors that they did not know how I lived through such an ordeal, but I knew."[2] Jane wanted to live, and she received help that made her survival possible.

Initially, Jane was uncertain what had happened to her, stating, "Whether she was an angel who had materialized to help or a human being, I don't know."[3] Later, however, conviction replaced the uncertainty. "I firmly believe the woman was an angel who manifested in physical form to help me," she told me. "I don't know if you can really create physical beings that you can touch, feel, and hear just by thinking it. Besides, I had just prayed for help, and it was answered immediately."[4]

Jane said she was in no position to have helped herself. She was panicking and struggling to breathe and didn't really know what was wrong with her. "I had no true understanding of the situation to give the proper solution," she said. "I definitely would have died. I thought I WAS going to die without understanding quite why, and panicked. I am sure I did not create the events."[5]

THE FACT IS THAT BENEVOLENT BEINGS, or at least something that is manifest as a being, are performing everyday miracles, saving lives, staving off loneliness, offering advice, and providing a balm to those who are grieving, to victims, and to those in the throes of disease.

I don't think the frequency—indeed the *normalcy*—of this experience should be understated. This is something that has happened to a great many people, people who in many cases have overcome a reluctance to share their experiences for fear of being stigmatized. Many harbor a hope that their stories will inspire others.

On the one hand, the sensed presence would seem to be an innately human capacity. That would explain its frequency, the very different sorts of people it has touched, its variety of forms, and the diversity of causes. Each eyewitness gives an account of an unseen being that helped to encourage, console, or, in some instances, intervene to save them. On the other hand, many of those who have experienced the presence don't see it as a human capacity at all; they have no doubt that the source of their survival was spiritual. It may be something we generate, but then it may also be something that we apprehend. The word that is often associated with this experience is angel.

We already know that people with religious affiliations and spiritual beliefs have certain advantages. For example, regular churchgoers live longer than those who rarely or never attend church services, suggesting advantages with respect to "stress, coping resources, and other health behaviors."[6] Adolescents with religious beliefs are already making better lifestyle choices; for example, they are less likely to smoke cigarettes or marijuana or drink alcohol, and they are more likely to wear seat belts and eat vegetables.[7] In fact, "religiosity/spirituality is associated with lower blood pressure and less hypertension; better lipid profiles and immune function."[8] Those with spiritual beliefs also overcome grief more quickly after the death of a loved one: they are simply more resilient. A study of relatives and close friends of patients with a terminal illness found that "absence of spiritual belief is a risk factor for delayed or complicated grief."[9] There's an obvious logic to that: those who possess a faith have a structure for dealing with the end to a human life and a context for an afterlife. But is it possible that spiritual belief not only helps people to cope with the death of someone close to them but also protects them from harm?

Many people do believe that angels intervene on their behalf. A 2011 Associated Press-GfK poll showed that 77 percent of American adults believe angels are real. The percentage is highest among evangelical Christians, but a majority of non-Christians also said they think angels exist, as did four in ten people who do not attend church services.[10] The poll is interesting, but it is not simply that people like the idea of angels. Other research shows that people say angels actually have assisted them in concrete ways. The Baylor Religion Survey (2007) found that a majority of all Americans believe that they have received help from a guardian angel at some point in their lives, with 55 percent agreeing with the statement: "I was protected from harm by a guardian angel." Women are more likely to report such an experience, at about three in five women, compared with one in two men. Perhaps most striking is that one in five Americans surveyed who describe themselves as having "no religion" claims that a guardian angel has protected them.[11] According to Christopher Bader, then-director of the Baylor Survey of Religious Values and Behavior, "If you ask whether people *believe* in guardian angels, a lot of people will say, 'sure.' But this is different. It's experiential. It means that lots of Americans are having these lived supernatural experiences."[12]

The idea that angels and other supernatural entities intervene in our affairs is universal. People around the world believe in angels and profess to have one assigned to themselves. The ground is particularly fertile in the United States. According to Scott Draper and Joseph O. Baker writing in *Sociological Forum,* "The notion that angels exist and are readily available to intervene ... is promoted by advocates and adherents from a broad range of religious traditions ... ranging from Catholicism and Protestantism to the 'New Age.'" One in ten Jews also claims to have had direct help from an angel. In fact, angelic belief is so strong in the United States that one academic study concluded it is an "American folk religion."[13]

Whatever this angel effect is, it must be taken seriously for the simple reason that it has the potential to touch any one of us.

FOURTEEN-YEAR-OLD SUSAN MORRIS had a tough, chaotic childhood, in and out of juvenile care. When her father threatened to return her to state custody, Susan ran away from home.

She called a friend, and they met up in a dangerous area of their town that was infested with drugs and crime. Her friend said he would help her find a place to stay. But as soon as Susan arrived, he told her to get into a car with some of his friends, that they'd meet up later. This was not the case.

Instead, Susan was driven to a crack house. There, one of the men started to hit on her, and when she resisted, he pushed her onto a filthy mattress where another man lay sleeping and began a sexual assault that lasted hours. She was repeatedly raped. At various times her rapist held a gun to her head and pulled the trigger, laughing at the click of the empty chamber. The fourteen-year-old believed she would die.

About an hour into her ordeal, however, Susan's mind seemed to clear and then focus on something of which she knew her assailant was unaware: the tangible presence of another being. It appeared suddenly, when the gun was placed against her temple. She could not see anyone but recalls that "the most wonderful and indescribable feeling overcame my entire body and being. That feeling was of great comfort, and the best word to describe it is love."

Susan then heard a voice, communicated to her mentally rather than audibly, and it was "very calm and loving and feminine." The words were at once simple and profound: "You will be okay." She felt to her core that what was being said to her was the absolute truth and that "even if I tried to doubt it, I would not be able to." It was not her assailant who was in control; after all, there was some other power present.

The encounter with this unseen presence lasted only a few minutes, and she knew instantly when it had left, as the loving voice was silenced and the physical sensation of another being ended. "I became quite distraught and actually mourned the loss of the presence because it was so wonderful, and I was thrown back into reality and the cold horror I was enduring." The assault upon Susan continued throughout the night, and although Susan remained upset that the presence left, she was now utterly without fear.

Her ordeal finally ended around five in the morning. As he dressed, the rapist, himself a teenager, urged his friend, who had slept through the assault and had only just woken up, to also rape the girl. The second man got on top of her but only pretended to assault her, whispering in her ear that she should play along so he didn't have to really abuse her to satisfy his friend. A short time later the two men left. "I remember crying very loudly, I think in part because of the intensity of what I had been through and partially because I hoped someone would hear and take pity on me and get help. I didn't know where I was and felt afraid to leave the room I was in."[14]

Someone must have summoned the police, who eventually did arrive, but Susan did not tell them about the attack. Further, despite the fact that she was a distraught, physically hurt, underage girl in a crack house, they did not ask if she was hurt or whether anything was wrong. However, her parents had reported her as a runaway, so instead of treating her as a victim, the officers placed handcuffs on her and took her to juvenile detention. She remained there for several months before being transferred to a children's home. "I remember feeling like I was responsible for the rapes because I had been a 'bad girl' since I was disobedient and had run away from home. I had very low [self-]esteem."

Later, as an adult, she disclosed the sexual assaults to her mother, boyfriend, and a few close friends, but she did not share the encounter with the presence with any of them. "It was so profound for me. I did not want others who maybe couldn't comprehend it to try and diminish it at all," she said.

Even now she is reluctant to speak with friends, in part because "I cannot sufficiently convey how powerful and amazing" it was but also because many of her closest friends are agnostic or, in a few cases, atheists. Although Susan does not consider herself at all religious, "and I share many of their philosophies," she has no doubt regarding the origin of the presence: "I imagine they would disregard my experience as a neurological/chemical reaction to the shock and stress I was under. I completely understand that rationalization. But I disagree."

The encounter provided her "with amazing strength and motivation"—and not only on that night. For, despite the disadvantages of her upbringing, Susan went on to obtain a law degree, and she attributes her subsequent success in life "to the memory of that experience." Over the years she has had other tremendous challenges to overcome, situations that left her "emotionally broken," yet not once since that night has she felt even a tiny fraction of what came over her; the presence has never returned to her. In a way its absence has only underscored the wonder of what happened.

Susan reflected, "It is very strange to say this, but if I had a choice, I would prefer to endure the awful experience I went through in order to live my life with the spiritual awareness I gleaned from the encounter."

STARTING WHEN HE WAS twenty-three years old, Arthur Agnew began drinking heavily. It started as a social activity: he would go with friends to the pub in his hometown "and drink and drink and drink." For the first five years he was able to balance the heavy drinking with the rest of his life, at least to a point. He and his wife had children and built a family, and Arthur had steady work as a security guard. Soon, however, he started to drink on the job and was heading down the path to full-blown alcoholism. As Arthur put it: "You don't know where the line is, and you cross over it. It's other people who know you have crossed it. It was way out of control."

The drinking escalated after he and his young family relocated to Livingston, a city outside of Edinburgh. He tended to stop visiting the pub and just stayed at home and drank. It was, he said, "a cheaper alternative." He would have six beers in the morning, just to start the day, and continue drinking throughout, sometimes adding shots into the mix. All semblance of a normal homelife was lost. Arthur couldn't hold down a job, and they survived on welfare. His health was also suffering: he had an enlarged liver as well as other problems associated with alcoholism. His first priority was not his health, however, or job, paying the bills, or his family—it was the alcohol.

His young boys were being badly affected. They didn't want to go to school. Social workers intervened. After a series of meetings Arthur was told that unless he mended his ways, the children would be taken into care. But even that threat was not enough to make him stop. "The kids were not the priority," he said. "This disease of alcoholism made itself number one in my life. Nothing else mattered." The boys were eventually seized, and yet that dramatic loss failed to alter his course, as, he stated, "My attitude was this gave me more time to drink, it gave me more money to drink as well."

He suffered blackouts. Sometimes he would be injured while inebriated and would end up at the hospital. Other times he would find himself in police custody as a result of being drunk and disorderly or being a nuisance. In court a judge told him: "You know what your problem is, Mr. Agnew. You have to stop drinking."[15] But judges were not the only ones who told him to stop drinking. So did his parents, social workers, and doctors. He even spoke to a priest. Everyone who was witness to the slow-motion wreck that was his life delivered the same message. "They tried to explain to me this was going to kill me; they asked me to quit for my sake, for the children, for the family. But I did not," said Arthur. "I had spoken to all these professionals, and none of them could help me. I was deaf to what they were saying."

Then the social workers sought to remove the children permanently and find an adoptive family for them. The boys were very young, and they had never experienced a normal upbringing on account of the drinking. Arthur was in no position to raise the children. It was July 1991, and Arthur was sitting alone at home. The television was off. He had finished one can of beer and was about three-quarters of the way through a second. He was staring out the front window at a streetlamp.

Then he suddenly felt "a presence" in the house with him, as if there were another person there with him, and he heard a voice. It was a male voice, and it spoke very clearly and with great authority, using a "no-messing tone." The presence said to him: "If you take another drink, you won't see out the year." The voice came over his shoulder, but Arthur didn't jump. He wasn't frightened. He did not turn around. He just turned his eyes to the floor. There was nothing else. The presence left, and he felt he was alone again.

Its message was something he had been told many times before but, he said, "I knew this was it. Everything made sense at that moment. I was really just a dead man walking. I was sick of being sick. I didn't finish that can of beer." Instead, he poured it down the toilet. Within two weeks he stopped using the Valium—the "dry alcohol"—he was also taking. Valium was actually part of the treatment to help him through his initial withdrawal from alcohol; however, it also quickly became an addiction, as he abused the tranquilizers as a substitute for alcohol when he ran out of money. One day, however, he just forgot to take one of the pills, and nothing happened: he had no reaction, so he skipped another one, then stopped entirely. He explained, gesturing over his shoulder: "I put it down to the guy here [the presence] as well."

"Was it God, or an angel? Was it my soul crying out? Did it come from deep, deep within me? I have no idea." The presence was emphatic, however, and its message was a command, one he felt he must obey. Arthur never doubted it, stating, "It was almost as if someone, the voice, knew me intimately. I felt a release, and a thought crossed my mind: now I can go forward."[16] The intervention saved his life. He began attending Alcoholics Anonymous meetings, which helped, but when he shared his own story, he held back about the presence. "I was afraid it would be attributed to an alcoholic hallucination," he explained. "I did not want to share it with anyone. It was a very, very powerful and private moment." He said of his ability to break the cycle of alcoholism: "It was a shock to me, to the social workers, to everyone." Arthur was able to regain custody of his children and reunite his family. He bought a cab and began rebuilding his career. He took up skydiving and has made some six hundred jumps. In 2007 he traveled in a MiG aircraft to the edge of space, eighty-two thousand feet. He has not touched alcohol or Valium again in over two decades. After his encounter with the presence, he has, in short, never looked back.

THE SUN HUNG LANGUIDLY over Cellito Beach in New South Wales, with the scorching heat dancing on the buff sand. Durwin Keg had been surfing for an hour and a half with a couple of friends and was waiting two hundred meters offshore for the next wave. Suddenly a pod of dolphins streaked past them. These were experienced surfers who knew that the presence of a shark would often agitate dolphins. Two of Durwin's friends were then able to catch a wave that carried them safely toward shore. But Durwin found himself alone on the deep blue water, counting the seconds until, he assumed, he would also ride a wave into shallow water.

Then he noticed a huge dark shape in the water. It appeared still, so he thought for a moment it might be a large clump of seaweed, but then it began to move toward him slowly. He felt the bottom drop out of his stomach as the realization sank in that it was a great white shark. He was too far from land, and the enormous predator was closing in on him. When confronted with great danger, we instinctively do a mental calculation: Is it possible to get out of this? What are the odds? He did the same, concluding that he had "absolutely no chance of surviving."

Durwin turned his surfboard to face the shore. If he was going to have one last look at anything, it was going to be his friends and the land in the distance. He made one paddling stroke, lurching forward slightly. The shark swam beneath his board, arcing around at lightning speed so that it was behind him, and then came directly at him, knocking him off his board and into the water. Another surfer, Michael Lawrence, was six meters closer to shore. "When I heard him scream I thought he was joking," Michael said. "Then I heard a scream of terror." He turned to see a massive fin, and Durwin thrashing in the water.

Durwin punched, kicked, pushed—did everything he could to ward off the shark, and he succeeded temporarily. Clambering back onto his board, he began paddling frantically, screaming more warnings to those on the water. He looked back and saw the shark again swimming straight for him, moving like a fat torpedo. The creature breached two meters away. It was massive, at least three times his own width.

Durwin then threw himself off his surfboard and tried to use it as a shield. The shark dragged the surfer some distance, and Durwin somehow found himself briefly on its back before the shark again dove. Durwin resumed paddling, but his arms and neck were stiff, and he struggled to put any distance between himself and his attacker. At one point the shark breached right beside him, so close he was able to look it in the eye. He felt he could see its utter ruthlessness.

It then went under and made another turn, readying to resume its attack. At that point Durwin gave up. He felt he had no strength left to fight: "He was going to eat me this time for sure. I resigned myself to the fact that I was already dead."

Then, suddenly, everything seemed to change. Time seemed to be suspended.

Durwin became aware of the presence of another being with him and felt it was "much stronger than one person." His panic and fear seemed to wash away, and he was left with a sense of peace and euphoria. "I had no fear whatsoever," said Durwin. "I was completely conscious of what was going on … but at the same time I felt as if I didn't exist." A strong voice urged him to get as close to shore as he could and he resumed paddling, now strongly.

The shark again came up behind Durwin, but this time it remained about a meter away. "I had no fear whatsoever and calmly but determinedly paddled," he said. The great white shark followed for at least thirty meters, then veered off. Durwin has since tried to understand what happened, and some people have told him that reaching that point of fearlessness was the key to his survival. He believes his lack of fear caused the shark to break off the attack.

He feels that he had encountered a spiritual being—an angel—that day. "When I got to that moment, calm and peace and complete acceptance of what was to come," he said, "it was totally divine intervention." He credits the angel with saving his life. "I shouldn't be here," he reflected. For the simple reason that he had experienced it, nothing anyone could ever say or do could dissuade Durwin Keg of the idea that an angel or some other spiritual being had intervened.[17]

MANY OTHERS IN THE PAGES that follow have the same conviction. There are rich and ancient traditions in Judaism, Christianity, and Islam that support that. Mike Aquilina, author of *Angels of God,* says such cases can be readily explained by a quick survey of what is known about angels, which he describes as "the pure spirits created by God to be our companions and helpers in this life, and who aid us in our quest for holiness."

Says Aquilina: "Each of us has a guardian angel smarter than 1,000 Einsteins, stronger than the offensive and defensive lines of the Pittsburgh Steelers, and created by God specifically to serve us." He said God has assigned us our guardian angel, "And it's up to us to call on him, to build a relationship with him."[18]

Angels as messengers of God may exist or they may not exist. That is not a demonstrable point; rather, whether they are real is something that resides in the realm of personal belief. But angels as guardians do exist. This book serves either as proof of the existence of guardian angels as heavenly representatives that watch over us or can be summoned to our aid, or as proof that something akin to guardian angels exists as a product of our mental processes, something so vivid, so dramatically helpful that they should not be doubted. People who experience the sensed presence are not literally swept up by a supernatural agency with wings, but they might as well be.

In 2010 a group of researchers in Montreal set out some fundamental properties of the sensed presence, noting first that it is "always *apparent*, that is, the sensation is always recognizable and independent of whether other cues are available."[19] Second, the sensed presence is "*localized* in space" in relation to the person who is experiencing the phenomenon; that is, they know the presence is "there"—at a specific location, often at the periphery of vision. Third, "the presences have some sort of *intentionality*, they exist in a particular relation to the subject." Finally, the paper adds that they are *spontaneous*, appearing suddenly.

All of these properties are usually present, although other cues, auditory and/or visual, are also sometimes reported. Rather than a vague impression, some people can actually describe who their helper is, sometimes reporting that it took the form of an angel or religious entity, but for other people it can be a deceased family member or a mysterious, compassionate stranger. And quite frequently communication is established, not of a kind that others would overhear, but a communication just the same.

Traditionally, scientists have labeled sensed presence experiences as hallucinations or delusions, and these experiences "are studied only insofar as they are associated with particular neurological or psychiatric conditions."[20] Yet there is not only a growing body of neurological research that suggests the brain has the ability to create the sensed presence but also psychological interpretations that theorize that in fact the mind is in one way or another responsible. In either case, some of this work suggests that experiencing a sensed presence performs a useful, if little recognized, function. It helps people cope. Not only, then, do some theories suggest an organic basis for the phenomenon; they also imply that it is a human capacity; it's possible that we create it for ourselves. This is a serious enough possibility that it has started to attract the attention of scientific researchers.

What's behind these sensed presence accounts? There are many theories.

One psychological explanation advanced for the sensed presence is based on the premise that it is brought on by absence. This is linked to the widow phenomenon, where the death of a loved one (and it is not always widows who experience it) feels the distinct presence of the departed. Nancy Reagan has experienced this with the late president. Another explanation posits that messianic ecology may have a role— in effect, that the presence is induced through a process of subtle suggestions and expectations among believers, most often in various religious contexts. Then there's American psychologist Julian Jaynes's notion of the bicameral mind, in which a more primitive command voice of the right hemisphere overwhelms the higher left-brain functions, a sequence of events that can be produced by stress.

There are even more neurological explanations than there are psychological. One proposes that the sensed presence is a misattribution caused by the brain's agency detection processes, a survival response that scans for clues that predators and enemies are nearby, and as such is part of human beings' biological equipment, stating, "the sensed presence is the experiential component of a threat detection mechanism that gives rise to interpretive efforts to find, identify, and elaborate sources of threat."[21] Then there is a theory that relates to a conflict that occurs between the brain's executive function—that is, its higher capacity for reason—and "low road" emotions; in essence, different parts of the brain respond to severe stress differently and vie for supremacy, with the sensed presence being an illusory byproduct. There's also a theory that the presence is simply the left hemisphere's attempt to explain right hemisphere anomalies. Lastly there is the possibility that, when under severe stress, the temporo-parietal junction produces strong distortions of the conscious self that in turn create the sensation of a fully externalized being.

That last theory is the only one for which any empirical evidence exists, as a case was observed in a clinical setting. From this example, involving a woman in Switzerland, researchers extrapolated that people in such situations are experiencing not a breakdown in the sense of a failure to function, as in a car breakdown, but instead a breaking down of the usual rules of how the body is represented in the brain. This in turn creates an externalized self that mysteriously behaves very much like an angel—and, indeed, many people consider it to *be* so—which comforts and strengthens them and has the potential even to intervene directly to protect them. According to this theory, however, they are only looking after themselves.

So there are plenty of scientific theories and a little, as yet inconclusive, evidence to suggest a neurological basis for the sensed presence. But there is no general agreement over what brain processes account for it and, more to the point, how it can take on beneficent properties. As psychologist J. Allan Cheyne said, "The vivid and compelling nature of the companion experiences, despite their elemental simplicity, likely cannot be overstated. Such experiences are almost invariably described as utterly compelling, far too vivid and real to be mere hallucination, which is usually to imply that it defies naturalistic explanation."[22]

Which brings us to that other possibility: that the sensed presence represents a real encounter with some actual entity or being—an angel. In this book I will look at this possibility along with all the others. For although it may sound ridiculous to secular ears, it is the conclusion that a good many of the people I spoke to for this book came to. Although some of them are familiar with one or another of the neurobiological or cognitive theories, ultimately they find them unconvincing, as the experience itself carries a curious authority. It is what the great psychologist William James, talking about religious and spiritual experience, termed "noetic": a form of meaningful knowing.

For many of these people there is no contradiction here.

David Janssen, who at age twelve experienced a presence during a terrible fire in an apartment and was saved by the intervention, put it this way: "Even if there are chemicals at work activating parts of the brain, it would make sense that a guardian, or God, activates them into specific action with a specific path out. How else would He communicate if not by the brain He has made?" For Janssen, God has given us an angel switch, a way to beckon help when it is most needed.

One thing is certain: people are having these experiences. They are real events in consciousness that happen to real people, in more situations than we might imagine. If this book tells the story of the angel effect—of those who have experienced a caring and proactive sensed presence in their lives—it also tells the story of our own need to find explanations when maybe it is enough just to acknowledge a simple idea, one that has been a part of human experience from the earliest times: we are never alone. It took me until the end of my research before I understood that I was also telling this story. In our neurobiology-obsessed age, it may be the one we most need to hear.

# - 2 -

# THE RWANDAN BISHOP AND THE BROOKLYN RABBI

## MESSIANIC ECOLOGY

IN ITS REPORT ON THE 1994 RWANDAN GENOCIDE, TI-
tled, "Leave None to Tell the Story," Human Rights
Watch described a killing campaign that "struck with a speed
and devastation that suggested an aberrant force of nature."
The trigger was the death of the country's dictatorial president, Juvénal Habyarimana, whose aircraft was shot down
near Kigali International Airport by a surface-to-air missile
on the evening of April 6. The incident was the spark needed
to ignite the fuel of hatred spread by Hutu Power, an extrem-
ist movement that included key figures in the country's elite.

Rwanda is one of the poorest and most heavily populated
nations in the world, a country rent for decades by ethnic di-
visions between its majority Hutu people and minority Tutsi.
The Hutu feared the impending implementation of a negoti-
ated power-sharing arrangement, the Arusha Accords, with
rebels from the Tutsi-dominated Rwandan Patriotic Front.
Tensions had been mounting for months, but with the death
of Habyarimana, the extremists seized their opportunity to
blame his death on the Tutsi opposition.

The Presidential Guard and other elements of the country's military and police as well as Hutu militia led in mass
killings of Tutsis, but tens of thousands of others, ordinary
people incited by their leaders and the hate media, quickly
joined them. "Like the organizers, the killers who executed
genocide were not demons or automatons responding to in-
eluctable forces. They were people who chose to do evil,"
wrote Human Rights Watch.

It was a well-organized genocide. Whereas bands of thugs
randomly killed some of their Tutsi victims as well as some
moderate Hutus, very quickly lists of target names began to

be distributed to the killers. The slaughter was conducted with the sort of thoroughness characteristic of government census collectors. They literally went door to door, sometimes with a clipboard in hand. They kept regular business hours, suspending the killing to go home in the evening to their families. Then they would get up the next morning and go back to the work of massacring people.

The slaughter intensified as the killers descended on large groups of people who sought refuge in churches, schools, and hospitals. They lobbed grenades into these sanctuaries, chased down victims, sometimes cutting their tendons so they could not escape, then returning later to finish them off. It's estimated that twenty thousand people were killed within the first five days. The pace of the killings then increased.

It did not let up for three months, at which time somewhere between half a million and eight hundred thousand were dead.

The individual horrors that make up that large number are so shocking as to be hard to comprehend. Human Rights Watch recounted how people were rounded up and herded into a church, which was then bulldozed, flattening "both the church and the people inside." One woman, a Hutu with a Tutsi husband, watched as her children were killed. The youngest, aged three, cried out, "Please don't kill me, I'll never be Tutsi again." He was then killed anyway. Elsewhere the body of a young girl lay on a road, "flattened by passing vehicles to the thinness of cardboard." Not all were killed quickly, however; some people had their legs cut off and were left to bleed to death.

Among those targeted for death was Bishop Alexis Bilind-abagabo, who was living at Kigeme, an old missionary station of the Church of England, when the genocide began. The mission consisted of a cathedral, hospital, secondary school, and assorted support buildings and residences, all spread over three hills. Not long after he became aware of the first killing—a young man whose corpse had been brought to the hospital—Bishop Alexis saw large numbers of wounded and others streaming in. From the mission he could see, by the burning homes left in their wake, the pattern of attacks the militia had launched. He realized the killings were of a systematic nature. Refugees were gathered in the main hall of the school. Soon three hundred people huddled there in terror.

In the midafternoon of April 10 a gang of the killers loitered across the street. Three of the young men were then sent to scout out the school. Alexis watched them approach, and he went out to meet them. He noticed that they hid their weapons.

"Bishop, we are coming to warn you that in a few minutes you'll be killed," one of the young men said. "The militia are coming to kill you." Alexis looked at them without fear and replied, "There are angels protecting us and surrounding this place. They will not allow you to kill us."[1]

The three left, but after thirty minutes he could see them approaching again, this time with others. When they reached a certain spot, he heard whistles. He assumed it was a signal to begin an attack, to which the Bishop and the refugees would have been unable to offer any resistance. Instead, the whistles seemed to summon the gang away. Subsequent approaches were similarly rebuffed at that same point. Alexis then realized that it was "the very spot where I had talked to the three boys about angels. ... Each time people came to attack, no one ever passed that spot."

The bishop had no idea what made him say that there were angels defending the school. "In actual fact," he said, "I just said it without much thinking, but there *were* angels disarming all the evildoers coming to us. This is something that went on for three months. If it was that day alone, probably I would have doubted, but then this was done in different ways several times."[2]

Later, as the threats grew even more ominous, several government and senior military officials showed up to advise everyone at the mission to travel to the region's administrative headquarters at Gikongoro, which was seven kilometers away. They argued that they could offer no protection at the mission, but at Gikongoro they would join thousands of other refugees under official protection. A large group decided to go, but the Bishop, his family, and a smaller group opted to remain at Kigeme. "God has called me to serve him here," Alexis explained. Two days later he watched as police escorted the refugees away. A week later all of those people— together with hundreds, perhaps thousands, of others—were slaughtered.

Bishop Alexis was living with his wife at a house next to the school. It was safer than his own, which was farther from the main mission buildings. During subsequent weeks he learned of the deaths of many members of his extended family. So many people had been killed that he felt it would be easier if he himself died, and he felt ready for that. Better that than to live in the charnel house that Rwanda had become.

Soldiers then appeared at the mission, recording the names of those left alive. Alexis saw three of the soldiers pass by his window and go to the neighboring house of another

Anglican clergyman who, weeks earlier, had moved to Kigeme from Gikongoro. After a short time the man emerged to tell Alexis that the soldiers wanted to speak with him. The heavily armed men then explained, "We want to take you to Gikongoro for questioning." Alexis knew those were code words for a death sentence. He said goodbye to his wife and got into the soldiers' vehicle. He accepted his fate, and felt at peace. But the jeep wouldn't start. After several minutes of trying, the soldiers ordered him out of the vehicle and, as they walked away, told him that they would come back for him later. They never returned.

Many of his belongings remained at his former house, and Bishop Alexis would visit it regularly. At some point the militia discovered this pattern and lay in wait for him. In late May he was inside when a voice told him: "Alex, you are in danger." He looked around, but there was no one else inside the house. The voice, however, was real and the message urgent. He quickly went outside and headed back toward the school. As he neared it, he saw a group of youths coming toward him. As soon as they saw him, they stopped, started laughing, and walked away. He understood the implicit message: "We shall have to kill you another day." The bishop estimates that the warning had come at just the right moment. "Within three minutes it would have been too late. … When God tells you danger is coming, you can feel it; you can really hear him."

Bilindabagabo recalled, "The voice was audible and clear to me, and immediately I obeyed. That saved my life, because I would have been killed in a few minutes. It is one of those times when you hear something but the person next to you does not hear it—a mental communication. I was very conscious of God's presence, and as time went on it became clearer indeed that God was present."[3]

Somehow, in the midst of a genocide that claimed so many, Bishop Alexis was, by some small miracle, spared. After the slaughter tapered off and the genocidal forces were put down, he asked himself: "Why am I alive?" Why was he alive when so many he knew were dead? It was not on account of his office, as other religious leaders were killed. Nor was it, he felt, because he was any more righteous than some of those who died so brutally. He believes he was spared for some purpose, and he has worked hard to rebuild and heal his country.

But as to the source of his survival, he has no doubt. Bishop Alexis Bilindabagabo encountered something of undoubted power during the Rwandan genocide. He was in a house of God and its ecology of belief. He believes it was due to the presence of angels, a force that stood sentry at the mission station at Kigeme. Hardly a day went by, he felt, when God with His emissaries had not done something to protect him and those who remained at the mission. It is a powerful good that can turn away a murderous army.

AFTER RABBI MENACHEM SCHNEERSON, the leader of the Habad-Lubavitch Hasidic sect of Orthodox Judaism, died in 1994 without leaving a successor, something very odd happened. It was business as usual for the rabbi, at least according to a significant number of his devout followers. Many refused to accept his expiration, claiming, "he continues to live, invisible but intact" at 770 Eastern Parkway, Brooklyn.[4]

References to the rabbi and his sayings are steadfastly maintained in the present tense. His residence, his office, his belongings are all kept as before—not as shrines but rather to reflect the belief that he remains to this day an active participant within the community. His photographic image is pervasive, and videos are regularly shown of him. His enduring presence is underscored by the rituals and as part of the daily routine. For prayers, the armchair belonging to the rabbi is uncovered for his use, and on the Sabbath and high holidays "congregants lift their eyes and gaze at the stairs descending from the rabbi's office on the second floor. Then they split to create a clear path … leading to the podium," as if making way for their leader.[5] In other words, the dead rabbi is treated as if he were physically present, "alive and well."[6]

All of this forms what Yoram Bilu, professor of psychology at Hebrew University in Jerusalem, terms a "messianic ecology." It is, he argues, the result of an elaborate interplay between expectations, iconography, and schedule, forming "an inviting, suggestion-saturated milieu for the Rabbi's presence." The use of photographs and videos contribute to a "strong cognitive schema" around the absent rabbi.[7]

Even during his lifetime some Hasids concluded Schneerson was the messiah, and this conviction only grew following what many consider to be his nondeath. "Cognitive expectation and emotional arousal are likely to supply the mindset and motivation for the proclivity to see the Rabbi," Bilu wrote. "But it is the constellation of concrete signs and markers of the Rabbi, and the practices in which they are embedded that structure the perceptional field in which the Rabbi can be seen."

In such an atmosphere it is perhaps unsurprising that many reports of the rabbi's presence have been logged. Yoram Bilu has documented seventy-six apparitions reported between 1994 and 2010. "All beholders reported they saw the Rabbi 'out there,' while fully awake, with their eyes open," wrote Bilu. He added that "Most apparition sightings are brief, ranging from a few seconds to a minute or two" and included a nonverbal gesture of encouragement or a short blessing. What is more, there is evidence that the rabbi can appear in the most unexpected places, as one witness observed, even in the home, "between the refrigerator and the kitchen sink."[8]

Many of the cases occur within the messianic ecology of 770 Eastern Parkway, the Habad-Lubavitch central headquarters. However, Bilu found they have also come from outside the United States, occurring in far-flung locales ranging from Australia to India and, of course, Israel.

Although the movement is currently experiencing an outbreak of such reports, it is not peculiar to Habad. Writes Bilu: "In a comparative vein, apparitions in ritual venues across the world, from visual encounters with the Virgin in Marian pilgrimage sites to Elvis sightings in Graceland, are likely to be associated ... where setting, expectations, training, and ritual may combine to produce extraordinary visual experiences."[9]

And yet not all the reports of Schneerson are where they might be expected, at such ritual venues. In one case the rabbi appeared in a laneway in the Israeli city of El'ad. A fourteen-year-old girl was en route from a community center to her home. It was close to 9 P.M. in May 2006, and she was hurrying down a path between a building and a field, when her leg got caught on what she thought was a rope. She stopped to free her leg, then realized it was not a rope at all but rather a snake. Terrified, she froze on the spot. She thought the snake would lose interest if she remained still. Instead, it wrapped itself more tightly around her leg. Her heart was racing. "It was gripping me with such strength that I started to lose sensation in my leg."

The girl didn't know what to do and started crying. She is a Habad, and "suddenly I saw in front of me, very close, the Rabbi." The presence communicated with her: "He looked straight at me, pointed down with his holy hand and said 'strangle it.' I don't know where I got the strength and the courage, probably the fact the Rabbi was right there in front of me gave me strength." She bent down and grabbed the snake near its head and began to squeeze with all her might. It remained firmly attached to her leg, but she kept pressing. Gradually the creature began to release its grip and then became limp. She at last heard "some kind of exhalation from the snake," which then dropped to the ground. She ran home, pale, her leg sore, but otherwise unharmed.

In 1999 Rabbi Schneerson was again reported, this time deep in the waters of the Red Sea. Shmaryahu Hagar was diving with some Israeli friends near Sharm el Sheikh, Egypt. A novice, his coach advised that he only descend to a depth of twenty meters, and then only with a partner. Somehow, though, during the descent he misidentified his partner and followed another diver who was going much deeper, to one hundred meters. At some point Shmaryahu realized something was amiss. He looked at his diving watch and discovered that he had reached a depth of forty-six meters. He was already feeling the effects of nitrogen narcosis, the so-called raptures of the deep, and soon after drifted into unconsciousness. He floated further down, like a leaf in autumn. Finally, he was jolted out of it when another diver swam after him and knocked on his mask; there was a second diver there also. The diver who had knocked on his mask was "making signs for me to go up immediately."

Shmaryahu did make it to the surface, where an Egyptian boat collected him and carried him back to the diving party. The diver who had saved him said that a trail of bubbles had alerted him but also that "something in me screamed that I must look for someone who is in distress. Indeed, when I went down I saw you had a problem. I don't understand how you survived, but you should know you were seconds away from getting to 80 metres." Shmaryahu then asked the man: "Who was next to you?" There was no one next to me, the man replied. "No way, I'm sure there was someone next to you," Shmaryahu insisted. After a couple of days it became clear to him who the second rescuer was; he recognized the other diver from a photograph. The figure was none other than Rabbi Schneerson.

Another case occurred in November 2001. Students taking a course in Jewish philosophy at a religious high school in Jerusalem were discussing evil and whether evil can be overcome. They soon had firsthand experience with the problem. A school bus carried a girl named Ilana and some of her classmates home that day. She sat with her head resting on the shoulder of a friend. The bus pulled up to an intersection in the French Hill, in northern Jerusalem, when a Palestinian man armed with a M16 stepped forward and started to spray the bus with bullets.

It was a horrific scene. In all, twenty-five people—most of them children—were wounded and two were killed, joining the list of civilian victims of the second Intifada. One of those killed was the girl upon whose shoulder Ilana had been resting her head. When the firing started, Ilana cried out for the rabbi. She too is a Habad, and the rabbi is someone adherents would appeal to in prayer. She had a sudden and powerful awareness that Rabbi Schneerson was there with her. According to her mother, "Ilana saw the Rabbi and felt him pulling her down to the floor of the bus, and so she was miraculously saved from the gunfire."

In each of these cases the stress was serious. Some involved life-and-death struggles. They may have been outside the messianic ecology of 770 Eastern Parkway, but nonetheless an apparition of Rabbi Schneerson intervened. If his presence was merely a product of deliberate manipulation, of subtle cues and the power of suggestion, of a carefully tended garden of expectation, then how did it happen during a Red Sea dive? Or in a school bus under attack? There were no videos of Schneerson there. In some situations a key factor is "serious distress and the emotional upheaval it entails. The threat to one's well-being in a context of Hasidic belief is sufficiently potent to engender a sighting even outdoors." So there is something more at work than an outbreak of visionary religious fervor among a movement with messianic tendencies that had lost its leader. "Acute and situation-specific stress" precipitated these cases, Bilu writes.

One possible explanation is a sort of messianic hangover. In this, if a person is immersed in such an environment, surely the impression that environment makes is not shed the moment they leave it; their expectations remain. In fact, their absence from their community and its supportive environment of expectation may intensify their search for cues. It is telling that, although they were outside the messianic milieu of 770, two of the three examples cited above involved Habad adherents. And the lone exception, the diver, was only able to identify his elusive second rescuer a few days later, once he had seen a portrait of the rabbi.

The feeling of a presence is at the root of many spiritual practices, in which it provides the experiential basis for belief. Messianic ecology feeds the expectation of such an apparition. One fascinating recent study of sensed presences, undertaken by researchers at the Dream and Nightmare Laboratory at the University of Montreal, makes the case that religious experience could not exist without it: "Whether one has actually felt the presence of the divine—or hopes to feel it—there seems to exist this vital need, curiosity or desire to experience the divine in this primal fashion."[10]

As with the Habads, ritual and expectation play a role in many faiths, whether with the sacrament of the Eucharist in Christianity or devotional objects in Hinduism in which the divine presence is believed to reside. "In many religions, the divine presence is symbolically enacted/produced ... and accounts of first-hand spontaneous encounters with the divine are numerous," wrote Elizaveta Solomonova and her colleagues at the University of Montreal. "Both religious and nonreligious individuals are attracted to built sacred places of worship, places linked to religious traditions, places where divine messengers were thought to have preached, places where revelations were experienced, or places where influential individuals were born or died."[11]

Habad's world headquarters in Brooklyn performs a similar function, then, as Marian pilgrimage sites, great cathedrals, and Hindu temples, with its "interplay of training, expectations, decor and schedule." As for the fact the rabbi is seen "in ritually unmarked settings, usually in harsh situation of acute danger"—this is consistent with the model of sensed presence.[12] It could happen to any person with religious belief when in distress.

Although people of differing faiths may not be exposed to anything approaching the messianic ecology that has been maintained around Rabbi Schneerson, many still tend to their own spiritual ecology and harbor a strenuous expectation that when unusual strain or stress and certainly great danger confronts them, they will be able to turn to God—or the Virgin Mary or their guardian angel—and find help.

It is this combination of factors that is so potent: beliefs and expectations coupled with stress and emotional arousal. As Bilu says: "Apparitions in which the Rabbi saved the seer from a life-risking situation share much in common with 'the third man factor,' an uncanny sensation of a mysterious presence that gives protection and guidance under grueling physical conditions."[13]

IN JANUARY 2009 reports of a miraculous apparition encountered in the course of a military operation in Gaza swept Israel. Israel launched the attack on the Palestinian territory in response to a barrage of Hamas rockets, and officials claimed that the targets would be confined to "the infrastructure of terror," principally Hamas fighters and weapons. Despite Israel's military advantage, it was still a dangerous and volatile situation on the ground. In the midst of it some young Israeli soldiers said they encountered an attractive woman who appeared several times in different places, issuing warnings. In one of the reports the young woman told a company of soldiers to avoid a particular building.

"Before we went in, we heard a voice," said Avner Azulay, one of the soldiers. "A woman's voice saying, 'Don't go in, there is death.'" He said the voice was heard just before they were about to enter. "We were ready to go in, we were by the door, but we were still outside of the house." Azulay gave an interview in which he attempted to describe what he had experienced. Here is a partial transcript of that exchange:

AZULAY: She said, don't go inside, there is death inside, and she repeated it many many times, until we thought that maybe … the problem was that she had no legs, no hands, and we couldn't see her face.

INTERVIEWER: What do you mean? I want to understand: you were seeing the woman …

A: Not a woman, some kind of image … a kind of white light, it wasn't connected to the ground at all. … I don't know how to explain …

I: So she was actually floating …

A: Yes, it was the image of a woman, but her face we couldn't see, she had no legs, no hands …

I: So you all saw it with your eyes; all of you.

A: Yes, it was this white light, it wasn't connected to the ground in any way … it was strange.[14]

The soldiers were in the midst of an operation and were on edge. A few tried to ask her questions, but she only responded to Azulay. Several of the soldiers made motions as if they "wanted to shoot her, as if she was a suspect or something." But Azulay intervened, telling the others to "give me a minute, let me ask her who she is." Immediately the woman said to him: "I am Mother Rachel."

Azulay told the interviewer that he is religious and recognized right away that it was Rachel, the Old Testament Jewish matriarch. "I realized it's not simple. ... I started to shake, I felt I am getting out of myself. ... No words can describe it, describe what I felt at that moment."

Although not all the soldiers shared his conviction, according to Azulay, the appearance of the apparition somehow seemed to paralyze them. "The truth, this was an incredible atmosphere; they were suspicious, but it was like when you have no strength to do anything. It was a strange situation, with all their weapons and stuff, they couldn't do anything."

But then they discovered the building was indeed "booby trapped with explosives; there was a wire from the door connected to the explosive in the house. Then we understood that she saved us." Azulay, out of shock, shouted, "Why did you save us?" And the woman answered, "For all the prayers that the people of Israel are praying, I was sent from above to save you."

Said Azulay: "And she disappeared like nothing. And I was left like this. To this day, I don't live normally, I can't get over it."

Rabbi Ovadia Yosef, who spoke with the soldiers, related how the "beautiful young woman" had also alerted soldiers to the presence of terrorists waiting to attack, telling them that "there were three armed terrorists waiting for them there."[15]

"Who are you?" one of the soldiers asked.

"What do you care who I am?" she asked, and then whispered, "Rachel."

The soldiers adhered to the mysterious woman's counsel. The rabbi described how the soldiers, when they did storm the building, indeed found and killed a nest of heavily armed Hamas fighters, just like the woman said. Thanks to her warning, the soldiers were spared. He and some of the others "alleged that a veritable miracle had occurred."[16]

"Mother Rachel was called to the place, 'Go save your sons.' Ah, praised be His name! God redeems and rescues, and sends angels to save the people of Israel. How we should thank God," Rabbi Yosef concluded.

A former chief rabbi in Israel, Mordechai Eliyahu, later revealed that he had prayed at the tomb of Rachel prior to the fighting, asking "that she ... beseech God to protect the Jews in the wake of an impending war." His clear implication is that his prayers had been answered.

Some in the media were skeptical, and others theorized that it was a religious hoax or "urban legend." Interestingly, one rabbi, Shlomo Aviner, disputed the religious explanation entirely, saying that "sometimes one is under pressure, tired, hungry, and thinks he sees something that isn't there."[17] The soldiers in question were young conscripts, doubtless experiencing stress. Azulay is a religious Jew, which may help explain his interpretation of the source of the help. One Israeli scholar, Gabriel Herman, identified the source of the apparition: "I would suggest that the soldiers experienced not a miracle but a psychological event—a sensed presence vision, which they identified as Rachel the Matriarch."[18]

IN 2011 HERMAN, professor in ancient history at Hebrew University in Jerusalem, published a study in
which he compared modern reports of presences—including
the experience of Avner Azulay and the other Israeli soldiers in
Gaza, Ron DiFrancesco in the World Trade Center, and third
man experiences among climbers and other explorers—to the
epiphanies of ancient Greece, such as Philippides's vision of
Pan, which he encountered while on a desolate, mountainous
path on Mount Parthenion. What Herman concluded is that
they are "slightly different manifestations of the same mental
process." In other words, what is happening today is precisely
what happened twenty-five hundred years ago and was responsible for the emergence of the entities that lent their name to
the concept of an epiphany—the sudden realization or com-
prehension of the larger essence or meaning of something. If
Herman is right, the sensed presence has always been with us.

According to Herman, most scholars view reports of the
ancient epiphanies with deep suspicion, believing them to
be the product of "superstitious fantasies or an overactive
imagination." Generally, these experts subscribe to social-
manipulation theory. A standard pattern is followed: "moti-
vated by sheer naiveté or by an explicit intention to mislead,
a highly superstitious, or a ruthlessly cynical person drops,
or plants, some remarks concerning a supernatural visitation
which he or she has dreamed up, imagined or invented. The
remarks are taken up and magnified by partisan believers,
and/or interest groups, through skillful manipulation of public opinion."[19]

Some of the visions of Rabbi Schneerson at 770 may apply
here, and Herman accepts that some ancient epiphanies

probably also fit this bill; they are conscious plants. However, he is convinced—and some other classical scholars share his view—that some epiphanies are true accounts of real experiences, the product of, as one put it, "mental states induced by … unusual physical and psychological conditions."[20]

For example, in 490 BC, during the Battle of Marathon, an apparition of Theseus, the mythical founder-king of Athens best known for slaying the Minotaur, appeared. Plutarch writes that "in the battle which was fought at Marathon against the Medes, many of the soldiers believed they saw an apparition of Theseus in arms, charging at the head of them against the barbarians." Herman argued that the soldiers "found themselves in an extreme life-threatening situation, being fully aware that they were outnumbered by a ruthless enemy." They believed their survival was due to interventions by a mythical being.

The second book of the Maccabees describes another, quite different case in 178 BC, after Simon, administrator of the temple in Jerusalem, quarreled with the high priest Onias and went to the king's governor to declare that the temple was full of unclaimed riches that could benefit the realm. In need of money, the king, Seleucus IV Philopator, instructed Heliodorus, his chief minister, to appropriate the treasure. When asked to turn it over, the high priest responded that the riches "had been deposited by people who trusted the dignity and inviolability of a world-famous temple and could not be confiscated." The chief minister insisted, however, causing great distress to spread among the population. People responded by filling the streets, calling upon the Lord Almighty to keep their deposits intact and safe. Then, "at the very moment when [Heliodorus] arrived with his bodyguard at the treasury, the Ruler of the spirits and of all powers produced a mighty apparition, so that all who had the audacity to accompany Heliodorus were faint with terror, stricken with panic at the power of God."[21] Heliodorus himself was stopped by three spiritual beings. He collapsed, and his men collected him and placed him on a litter. "This man, who so recently had entered the treasury with a great throng and his whole bodyguard, was now borne off by them quite helpless."[22] Again, Herman argues, the author of 2 Maccabees details "the distress that engulfed the city's population prior to the apparition." Even anxiety over money and finances can evoke beings.

Herman also cites the "many dangers" faced in 40–39 BC, when the Roman general Quintus Labienus launched a campaign of pillage through Asia Minor. Having laid waste to the region, at one point the general gathered his forces around the religious shrine at Panamara, near the modern-day village of Baðyaka in southwest Turkey. Three times Labienus launched attacks against Panamara, and three times apparitions diverted or repelled his forces. Labienus brought in reinforcements and tried one last time, but this attack was also rebuffed, and "a snarling as if of dogs attacking the assailants was heard" before the Roman soldiers were again repelled. They retreated, giving up the assault. Panamara's spiritual protectors prevailed.

Despite the gulf in time that separates our own world from the ancient world, Herman argued that these epiphanies as well as modern-day examples "do not constitute disparate entities … they belong, in fact, in the same analytical group by virtue of a psychological mechanism built into human nature." Both sets of visions—ancient epiphanies and modern sensed presences—were "preceded by a life-threatening trauma and/or a state of severe existential distress."

If you accept Herman's premise—if you accept, as he put it, "the sheer bulk of the evidence" that these cases reflect real experiences—then ancient epiphanies and the sensed presence are one and the same phenomenon. To ancient percipients Theseus did take up arms against the Medes, apparitions did drive Heliodorus from the temple, and, for modern witnesses, a guard of angels did protect Bishop Alexis, Rabbi Schneerson did save a diver from drowning, and Rachel did intervene to save Avner Azulay and the Israeli soldiers in Gaza.

As Herman said, with recent research into the sensed presence phenomenon, "we are making a small step towards bridging the gap between the biological and cultural aspects of that uncanny human phenomenon that is variously called visions, apparitions, epiphanies, phantoms, phantasma and hallucinations."[23] He argued that history needs to be revisited and historians' past practice of "discarding miraculous events and supernatural interventions" reconsidered. He said historians should start their investigations of past events "not from the externally visible, palpable 'great and marvelous deeds,' but from the neurochemical processes that took place in the minds of protagonists." That would change forever the way we see history.

THINK OF IT: people continue to experience today something that people have experienced since the earliest recorded times. Only the terminology has changed. The epiphanies became apparitions, and now the sensed presence. As Tim Cornell wrote in *The Beginnings of Rome*: "Reported sightings of divine beings at great battles—gods, angels, the Virgin Mary, etc.—are copiously documented, from remote antiquity to the First World War and beyond."

Today, angels, saints, the Virgin Mary, Rachel the Matriarch, God, and even Rabbi Schneerson have replaced the pagan gods or heroes of the ancient Greek religion. They have been present at battles from Dorylaeum to Gaza, and time and again through history, at other times of individual stress and often episodically, tied to great societal stress. They were in Mexico during the Spanish conquest, they were in England during the Norse invasions, they were in Spain during the plague years, and as we know from Ron DiFrancesco and other accounts, they were in the World Trade Center on 9/11.

In fact, Gabriel Herman has suggested that Emperor Constantine's vision of a cross-shaped trophy of light in the sky and the message "by this conquer" is also a sensed presence event. At the time of the vision Constantine was marching to put down a coup by his father-in-law. Failure would have been disastrous for him. Initially, Constantine thought the vision was the sun-god Apollo, but two years later it dawned on him that the sign was not pagan at all but instead came from "the God of the Christians." In AD 313 the emperor issued the Edict of Milan, ending persecution of Christians. Herman wrote, "We could assert, with a considerable degree of certainty, that one of the greatest religious revolutions in western history—the conversion of the Eastern Roman Empire from paganism to Christianity—owed its origin to a sensed presence vision."

In AD 452, in the midst of the barbarian invasions, with the Roman Empire in a state of collapse and barbarian armies wreaking havoc, two shining beings appeared during a meeting between Attila the Hun and Pope Leo the Great. This intervention purportedly caused Attila, the so-called scourge of God, to call off his planned attack on Rome. Church tradition has it that the interveners were Saint Peter and Saint Paul; the vision is depicted in a fresco by Raphael in the Vatican. The historian Edward Gibbon said the "apparition of the two apostles ... who menaced the barbarian with instant death if he rejected the prayer of their successor, is one of the noblest legends of ecclesiastical tradition."[24]

British scholar Kent G. Hare has produced a list of eighty-five examples of heavenly beings reported in medieval England and observes an evolution in the nature of the apparitions. In the beginning, he wrote, "celestial beings heal, console, protect, and chastise." As Hare noted, "the prototypes contain only ... benign apparitions." But by the end of the tenth century the ground shifts, with "apparitional beings administering punishment or participating in war."[25] Hare broke down the visions he collected from medieval England into five categories. More than half he classified as examples of "benign" interventions, with a smaller group serving as examples of "chastisement." Roughly a third, however, are categorized as "military counsel," "military defence" or "military offense." These angels can mean business. As a dramatic illustration of the imperative to keep on the good side of apparitions, consider the fate of Sweyn Forkbeard.

On February 2, 1014, Forkbeard, a Danish king and marauder, had gathered his army at Gainsborough, England. He was a formidable fighter and leader. His first campaign was waged against his own father, who was either driven into exile or killed in the uprising, depending on which account you believe. Later Forkbeard undertook a series of invasions of England, doing great damage in the process. This night, surrounded by his officers, Forkbeard "cast out threats" that he would spoil the nearby monastery where Saint Edmund the Martyr's sacred remains were interred. St. Edmund had been king of East Anglia and, after initially defeating the Viking warlords Hinguar and Hubba, was captured by them and tortured to death in 870. He was long dead. And yet on this day St. Edmund returned.

Accounts differ as to what happened. According to one, St. Edmund appeared to Forkbeard and "gently addressed him," Forkbeard, however, responded by mocking the saint, who then exacted a terrible punishment. Forkbeard "thought he saw St. Edmund coming all Armed toward him," according to Simeon of Durham. Terrified, he cried out vehemently: "Help, help, Fellow-soldiers, look here, King Edmund comes to kill me." As he uttered these words, Forkbeard "received a mortal blow by the saint's hands, and so fell from his horse, and lying till the dusk of the evening in great torment, he expired." He believed he saw the apparition of St. Edmund, and that belief scared him to death.

IT IS NOT ONLY MILITARY INVASIONS or threats that can prompt such reports. William A. Christian Jr. has documented many examples related to the spread of the bubonic plague in Spain. It was a time of crisis, with the epidemics rolling across Europe and creating an atmosphere of "constant anxiety, not only for the year-to-year survival of individuals and families but also for the survival of entire communities."[26] There was a commensurate spate of accounts of angels, the Virgin Mary, and other "apparitions instructing people as to preventative or curative measures." Sometimes these benevolent beings simply urged adherence to Christian practice and teachings. This was a genuine comfort to those whose world was collapsing around them as the plague stalked the valleys, fields, and villages. Devotion was armor against panic.

A well-documented example involved the August 3, 1458, visit of Our Lady of the Miracle to Lleida, an arid area of Catalonia dotted with semifortified farmhouses. At dusk two young boys witnessed the apparition at the same time as their father was helping to bury a neighbor girl who had succumbed to the plague. The neighbors had a second child sick at the time, and fear and alarm was gripping the area.

The boys and their mother were left behind to harvest wheat. Celedoni, the elder boy, was sent to get some mules, but on the way he encountered a "thing resembling a beautiful child" in a meadow. The mysterious child was kneeling about three paces from him, with its hands joined toward heaven, holding a cross. This figure spoke to him, saying, "O son, come here and tell the people." But the boy was frightened and ran away. He told his mother, Constança, who in turn went to investigate, but she herself was frightened and quickly returned without any information about the apparition.

Later, Jaume, the younger son, went the same way and "saw a being like a beautiful blond child, dressed, he thought, in a red cape." Both boys referred to what they encountered as "la cosa"—the thing. However, when questioned, Jaume, who was eight years old, thought it "seemed to be a girl ... because she had very long hair, like a woman, and blond." The girl was kneeling and had a cross on her shoulder. He walked up to within two paces of her, then the figure spoke to him: "Tell the people to make processions, and make them devoutly, and to confess and convert and return to the side of God, and that if they do, God will forgive them." She then arose, let him touch the cross, and kissed his hand. She walked away down a path and vanished.

The message from the girl was simple: "Devout processions would earn God's help. Disbelief would lead to certain, terrible punishment."[27]

So, Christian asked, "Is it a coincidence that Celedoni and Jaume saw a God-girl on the day their father went to bury a neighbor's girl dead of the plague, a girl they must have known?" The implication being the appearance of Our Lady of the Miracle in Lleida was a direct response to the terror that was afoot with the bubonic plague. The "thing," as the boys referred to it, was a source of hope and comfort to those faced with death. In fifteenth-century Spain there was a mass outbreak of such sightings, and, Christian argued, "the divine beings ... generally offered ways for the towns to avoid epidemic diseases."[28]

Such an outbreak of visions occurred again in Spain in April 1931. Once again the country was in crisis; this time the source was not epidemic diseases but instead the proclamation of a republic in Spain, the exile of the king, and anarchist and anticlerical attacks on the Roman Catholic church, together with the expulsion of the primate of Spain, Cardinal Pedro Segura. All of this created fear and confusion among many Spaniards.

Father Josemaria Escrivá, who founded Opus Dei and is now a saint, was one of those targeted. At the height of the anticlerical prosecution in Madrid "a would-be aggressor stood menacingly in Josemaria's path with the obvious intention of doing him harm. Somebody suddenly stood between them and drove off the assailant. It all happened in an instant. The protector came up after the incident and whispered to him: 'Mangy donkey, mangy donkey' the expression Blessed Josemaria used to refer to himself in the intimacy of his soul. Only his confessor knew about this. Peace and joy filled his heart as he recognized the intervention of his Angel."[29]

So many cases follow the same pattern, occurring all over the world during times of collective stress. In 1519 invading Spanish forces fighting the indigenous people of Mexico found themselves trapped in a perilous position, but they survived, attributing their survival to the appearance of Saint James, the patron Saint of Spain. St. James was witnessed "careering on his milk-white steed at the head of the Christian squadrons, with his sword flashing lightening [sic], while a lady robed in white—supposed to be the Virgin—was distinctly seen by his side, throwing dust in the eyes of the infidel."[30] Only a few years later the apparition of the Virgin Mary on the hill of Tepeyac in present-day Mexico City in December 1531 helped to calm those on the other side, a people whose land had been invaded and whose own religion had been shattered.

That is what also happened in La Vang in Quàng Trị Province, Vietnam, when in 1798, Catholics, hiding from persecution, saw a lady in a tree, accompanied by two angels. This time the Virgin "comforted them and told them to boil leaves from the trees for medicine to cure the ill."

On April 2, 1968, at El-Zeitoun, a district of Cairo, Egypt, two men saw a woman dressed in white on the roof of the

Coptic Christian church and, thinking she was going to commit suicide, contacted police. A crowd gathered, and many others saw the figure before she disappeared. The figure later returned, and, again, many witnessed it. The visions have been linked to the "tenuous position of Coptic Christianity in Egypt" and first appeared at El-Zeitoun months after Egypt's disastrous defeat during the Six-Day War.[31] "That defeat plunged Egypt into a state of national despair, and generated a great deal of anxiety about the future," wrote Michael P. Carroll in his book *The Cult of the Virgin Mary: Psychological Origins*.[32]

And then, on November 28, 1981, while in the dining room of a residential school run by nuns in Kibeho, Rwanda, seventeen-year-old Alphonsine Mumurek was startled when a voice addressed her as "my daughter." The girl looked and saw a woman of incomparable beauty and asked, "Who are you?" The reply was "Ndi Nyina Wa Jambo"—that is, "I am the Mother of the Word." This was the first apparition of the Virgin Mary at Kibeho, but other girls also reported similar visions in the months following Alphonsine's. The Roman Catholic Church established a commission of investigation, which concluded, "there are more reasons to believe in the apparitions than to deny them."[33]

At first the apparitions involved calls for penance and fasting, but the girls soon related more ominous messages. They spoke of horrific scenes of rivers of blood, severed heads, bodies abandoned without burial. Later, some considered the visions to have been a prophesy of the genocide that took place in Rwanda beginning on April 6, 1994. Among its many victims was one of the girls who had seen Our Lady of Sorrows at Kibeho.

A recent study found sightings of the Virgin Mary increased from a low of seventeen reports in the eighteenth century to over four hundred in the twentieth century, most of those in the last fifty years. Scholar E. Ann Matter wrote, "the striking fact is that the twentieth century, more than any other time in Christian history, has been the age of the cult of the Virgin Mary."[34] She noted studies that show "that between 1975–2000 there were, on every continent of the globe, an increasing number of apparitions." In fact, the frequency increased with each decade, so, for example, "far more are reported in 1997 than in 1987."

Apparitions of the Virgin Mary have been coming in fast and furious. There are so many, in fact, that the Vatican's Sacred Congregation for the Doctrine of the Faith in 1978 first issued a document, "Norms for Judging Alleged Apparitions and Revelations," and later, in 2012, translated those rules from Latin into English and other languages and published them online.

Record numbers of Marian apparitions? A majority of Americans experiencing guardian angels? Reports of Rachel the Matriarch in Gaza? An outbreak of sightings of Rabbi Schneerson? The world has changed a great deal in two thousand years, but in this one respect it has changed very little. So what is causing this rise in reports? One theory holds that it is evidence that our world is in stress. As Matter wrote in her study of Marian apparitions in the late twentieth century: "visions of the Virgin Mary are associated with particular times of cultural stress." A number of scholars have studied the phenomenon and also concluded that they are in part, a "response to the social and political tensions of our period of history."

Supernatural players have been active throughout history and to this day remain a tangible experience for a great many people. John Milton wrote in *Paradise Lost* that "millions of spiritual creatures walk the earth / Unseen, both when we wake, and when we sleep." That was in 1667. Evidently, for some, spiritual creatures are still walking the earth.

Just ask former FBI agent Lillie Leonardi, who, in the terror of the aftermath of 9/11, says she saw a legion of angels guarding the Pennsylvania site where United Airlines Flight 93 crashed. Leonardi recounts in her book *In the Shadow of a Badge: A Spiritual Memoir*, how a white mist gathered in the field and "I saw what appeared to be angels." Soon she was witness to a miraculous sight: "There were angels standing in the open area to the left of the crash site. There were hundreds of them standing in columns," Leonardi wrote.[35]

And just ask Bishop Alexis Bilindabagabo.

It is clear that the source of each vision's attribution is rooted in each person's practice. As Herman wrote, "sensed presence visions involve figures ... or vague, indeterminate, 'presences'—endowed, however, with some sort of supernatural powers—derived from the visionary's cultural or religious heritage." A Christian is not going to see Rabbi Menachem Schneerson or Rachel the Matriarch; a Habad is not about to report seeing the Virgin Mary, a saint, or Jesus Christ; and a Hindu is not going to see any of them, nor is a Buddhist. That is the power of culture and faith. Yet the underlying cause is another matter.

It is easy to imagine how a carefully cultivated and fertile environment for apparitions can in fact give rise to them in the midst of a genocide. Bishop Alexis was, after all, holed up in an Anglican mission, with its cathedral and rich Christian milieu. But he was also under immense stress with his life under threat at every turn, an atmosphere ripe for sensed presence experiences. You don't need the appropriate spiritual ecology for it to happen, nor do you need to be an active religious believer like Avner Azulay or a religious practitioner like Bishop Alexis Bilindabagabo.

There is no question that a great many people who experience a sensed presence assign it a spiritual identity, but not all. Indeed, the protective guardian's identity can sometimes be attributed to the most mundane of sources, some even confounding—like a Mexican cleaning woman.

# - 3 -

# THE

# MEXICAN

# CLEANING

# LADY

## PRESENCE BROUGHT ON
## BY ABSENCE

JOE LOSINSKI, A YOUNG U.S. MARINE FRESH FROM serving in Iraq, had ten days' leave before he was scheduled to rejoin his unit and redeploy. Recently married, he and his wife, Heather, decided to drive from Camp Pendleton, California, where he was stationed, to his hometown of North Pole, Alaska. Heather planned to remain in Alaska, and they intended to make a life there once his service ended. She needed a vehicle, so they decided to take their 2002 Chevy Cavalier to North Pole. Joe would spend a couple of days visiting family, then fly back to Camp Pendleton. Time was tight, so they decided to drive virtually nonstop, with only the occasional pit stop, taking turns at the wheel.

They set out in May 2004. Heather drove from Los Angeles to the Canadian border. Joe then took over the wheel and drove from the Canadian border to their final destination. The distance was 3,474 miles (5,591 kilometers). It was very ambitious, and, as Joe put it, "In retrospect I wouldn't have done it if I had realized how grueling it was, but we were fairly young, and I figured coffee and cigarettes would suffice."[1]

Well into their second day on the road they were both totally exhausted. Joe was driving and needed to remain in a state of heightened awareness, as the car was passing through a mountainous area in British Columbia during a spring snowstorm. To make matters worse, he was driving at night, with his wife curled up asleep in the passenger seat. Traveling at night during a heavy snowfall can have a hypnotizing effect on a driver. As the headlights illuminated the snowflakes as they whizzed past the windscreen, Joe was fighting the temptation to watch the dance of snow rather than concentrating on the road ahead.

He estimated visibility at under two hundred feet and had already had one close call when a large moose crossed the highway in front of the car. The animal had been so close that Joe could look into its eyes, which the headlamps had illuminated.

The snow, coupled with his heavy eyelids and the seemingly endless twists and turns of the mountain passes, had Joe anxious they were one bend away from a serious accident in the middle of nowhere. As he labored on, he became "aware that I was in a tenuous position and was increasingly nervous, even though I had driven in similar conditions growing up in interior Alaska." But then the anxiety gave way to a different state. "As I grew more fatigued," he recalled, "my anxiety lessened and I felt a sense of automation, for lack of a better word, like I was 'putting one foot in front of the other' and plodding ahead as I had done during long marches in the service."

It was then when he felt he began to receive help. "I don't recall when I first noticed 'her,' but I know that ... as I drove on a voice calmly gave me minute-by-minute instructions: 'Slow down around this turn,' 'Now back the other way, don't overcorrect.' I didn't see her in front of me as much as I was aware of her hovering just over my line of vision. I was unable to see the lay of the road and adjust accordingly. I was responding only to her commands."

Joe did not feel the commands were audible and did not respond to them verbally, but he has no doubt that there was communication. "She spoke, and I acted by heeding her instructions. Through her I was able to anticipate what the next bend in the road held and how to operate our car in a safe fashion."

This went on for several hours. What's more, Joe had an image of who was helping him: she was a middle-aged Mexican woman, "heavyset, with her hair pinned up neatly in a bun and wearing a cleaning lady's uniform—white apron, paisley blue dress with a collar, and flats. I didn't see her in front of me as much as I was aware of her in the upper part of my forehead, as though she was hovering just over my line of vision."[2] He felt she was a domestic worker. To this day he has absolutely no insight as to who she was, what made him think she was Mexican, or how he knew what she looked like, but he did have a mental picture of her just the same: "She resembled no one I knew, either physically or emotionally, meaning that I didn't identify her as a 'grandmother' type figure like one of my grandmothers." However, the sensation was so vivid that he felt he would recognize her if he passed her on the street.

The Mexican cleaning lady was not his grandmother, and yet he felt a sense of the sort of gentle authority that grandmothers can possess. "What struck me most during my experience was the serenity that the lady exuded; her commands were more akin to gentle admonitions like a grandmother coaxing a small child. 'You ought not do this' or 'You ought to do that, my dear.' I haven't experienced anything like that, before or since; I'm not sure if she was a guardian angel or simply a figment of my overworked psyche, but nonetheless she got me through the worst driving conditions of our trip unscathed."

After several hours the car emerged from the snowstorm and on to clearer roads as day broke. He told his wife, who had slept through the night, what had happened. They laughed it off as a sleep- and nicotine-deprived delusion, yet Joe continued to mull over the encounter. He couldn't really shake the idea that something profound had happened to him.

"I believe that were it not for 'her' I wouldn't have been able to navigate the roads and would have found it difficult to find a place to pull over. The most amazing thing to me as I reflect is that I didn't fall asleep at the wheel, which would have certainly resulted in an accident. It was as though I was constantly on the verge of passing out but never did. I'm convinced I have her to thank for that."

Joe grew up in a religious home and was well aware of spirits, angels, divine intervention, and the like, but when this incident occurred he was not suddenly "enlightened" and in awe of God's miraculous power; it remains a mystery to him: "Even now I suppose it is possible that it was God directly intervening in my situation, but I cannot rule out that it was a mysterious function of my brain in response to extreme circumstances. I hadn't experienced it prior to the incident and have not since."

THERE WERE A NUMBER OF FACTORS at play—exhaustion, monotony, stress—but one theory is that Joe encountered a sense of presence brought on by absence; that is, his mind had simply responded to fill a void of companionship with what Michael Shermer, in *The Believing Brain*, terms, "an extension of our normal sense of ourselves and others in our physical and social environment." After an intense couple of days together his wife was asleep, so although present physically she was effectively absent during a stress-laden few hours of driving. There was no one he could talk to, no one to help him stay awake, no one with whom to share his anxiety, and no one to give him helpful advice. We are a highly social species and crave company. When we are under duress the need for companionship intensifies. If human company is not available in such circumstances, the stress and anxiety deepen.

This fundamental human need is why one of the worst punishments our penal system can mete out is solitary confinement. Although many people now choose to live alone, there are still vestiges of the pity once assigned to men who remained bachelors and to "spinsters." And in fact, many studies have found that singles don't fare as well, either in terms of health or longevity, as do people living with a partner. One study suggested that married people on average live up to nine years longer than do singles.[3] That is an astonishing figure, but it would seem to support what is already known: we have a need for companionship, an expectation of others.

At one point or other, even if only just when we were children, we have all lived in the close company of other people. Yet there are some of us who will go home every day alone. And those people can experience profound loneliness. It is a deficiency state. It doesn't matter how many calls they took at the office, or if they had lunch with colleagues, or how packed it was when they took the subway home, they still enter an empty house. It is an act of arrival not unlike when they once came home from school, but instead of waiting parents or siblings, only silence greets them. In some cases the absence trigger is much fresher. They arrive, and instead of a partner who has recently moved out or has passed away, they discover again there is no one. Yet a remnant social impression of others remains. This is most acute after a sudden separation or loss, but that feeling can persist for years, sometimes decades. Disappointment lurks even when it has been forgotten. Even places can evoke the sense of a presence: "entering someone's house containing objects arranged in ways their owner intended can lead to a distributed but clear sense that the person is actually there" when they are absent.[4]

And when our very social nature is denied or suppressed, when we do not have real people around us, we can create them. Friendly, supportive unseen beings are very common, for example, among young children. Some studies have suggested about one in every three children between the ages of three and six has an imaginary playmate, although the better term is invisible friend, for they are not make-believe but instead represent real, lived experiences. Children converse with them, play games with them, can mimic their voices or even accents, and can become their closest friends even to the exclusion of other, flesh-and-blood children. And it is not surprising that invisible friends are most common among children who are lonely or under stress. And what is the stress? In some cases it is the stress of isolation or unwanted solitude, but in many it is the loss of a parent through divorce or death.

Most of these friendships last six or so months, but that is not always the case; some last for several years. There are even cases of childhood imaginary companions that persist into adulthood. In such instances the invisible friend "too grows up with the child and begins telling him or her what to do in times of stress."[5]

While undergoing counseling, a man named Peter, in his late twenties, admitted that he "admired and respected" an imaginary companion named Harry. Peter said he needed Harry "to survive and escape" and had a sense of security in having this "Harry image" around. He could even describe him: "Harry is about 40 years old, maybe, paunchy and dresses in a shapeless trenchcoat." The analyst reported that Harry was a help, noting, "Peter began to deal with the isolation and self-defeat that characterized his life through the creation of Harry ... Peter was able to feel more human, more alive, and ultimately, more of a man."[6]

Another case involved a woman who developed an invisible friend as her marriage began to fail. She described this friend as male, red haired, and younger. "I would usually talk to him when I was alone in the car and driving somewhere. ... I would tell him all the things we could do together in the area and all the sights he could see. I would explain about the local sights as we drove through town and the countryside. Once we stopped at a waterfall along the side of the road because I thought he might like to see it." She would keep the passenger seat of her car clear for him, and made CDs with her favorite songs to play for him. "I never talked to him about 'serious' or unpleasant stuff—I think I had enough of that in real life. ... I enjoyed our time together." The woman, who did not reveal her name, said her companion came "because I was very lonely. ... He was a companion during that awful 'stuck' phase of my life." When her marriage ended, the red-haired man stopped coming.[7]

ANTHONY BALEJ FELT AS IF HE WERE DYING a little bit every day. In fact, there were moments when he wished for it. He saw death as a release from a life he didn't want, a life he felt no longer had any value. After his wife left him he was in the trough of a deep depression, one that he felt he would not ever climb out of.

Anthony and his wife had celebrated the birth of their first child in 2005, and very soon after that the marriage failed. Anthony was left feeling bereft and unable to cope with single parenthood, and he was forced to move to another city in Texas in order to live with his parents. His father attempted to prevent the move, but his mother wanted to assist with the baby, who had health problems. The result was a serious rift in his parents' marriage, a schism that Anthony felt was the direct product of bringing an infant into their home. In the end his parents went through a divorce at the exact time he did.

At age twenty-five, Anthony had not only suffered through his own divorce, but he also felt responsible for his parents' divorce as well. His mother had a difficult time dealing with the end of her thirty-year marriage, and although Anthony didn't believe it was intentional, she took out a lot of her anger on him. He was trying to deal with his own heartbreak and raising his daughter. He felt very much alone, and often he was barely holding it together. He was consumed by guilt, pain, and anger. Instead of being a refuge for his daughter and himself, his childhood home became mired in quiet recrimination and despair.

Then he lost his job, a very well-paying and stable job, and the resulting loss of health insurance for his daughter compounded this blow. This situation became entrenched. Nothing changed, and nothing improved. Anthony felt that this was the life he was destined to live, a life he saw as worthless, lonely, and unfulfilled. "That I didn't just end it entirely was because I felt so guilty for how my daughter would grow up without her father," he said. "I was pretty much all she had."

In desperation, Anthony cashed out his $30,000 in savings, parked his daughter with an aunt, and bought a one-way air ticket to Asia. "I was running away from something that had become so horrible to cope with—my life—consequences be damned," he said. When he arrived, he backpacked through several countries and risked his life pointlessly several times. "I remember being robbed with a knife held to my throat. … I asked them not to kill me because my daughter had nobody to raise her if she lost me. It was all that came out. It was the only reason I had for living, which I only felt as an obligation rather than a desire. It's embarrassing looking back at it now. I had so little care for my own life."

One night he found himself in Ban Thana, Laos, well off the beaten tourist track. He had checked into a cheap hotel and had gone to his room. He had been enjoying the new cultures but still felt as if he were tethered to "an emotional ball and chain." In essence, he was "trying to buy my way out of my depression with the little savings I had left, but it was not working. My mind focused constantly on my own misery and self-pity." Yet something astonishing happened that night in Ban Thana. "The person I was died in that hotel room that night. That person has never returned."

Anthony turned out the lights, sat down on the floor, and began to cry. He had reached rock bottom. And that is when a presence appeared. It appeared suddenly, but it didn't scare him, even though he had never encountered anything like it in his life. When it spoke, it did so with authority. It gave the impression that it knew everything about his life and that he didn't need to explain anything to it.

Anthony had a conversation with the presence that lasted for fifteen to twenty minutes. He spoke to it and could understand the responses, but he said the voice was "not actually there making sound"; rather, he felt as if it were conversing with him mentally. "I remember some specific questions. I asked if I could die; it said that I was needed and that my life would have an impact on others. I could not discard it. I talked about some very personal things, and it talked openly and frankly about them with me."

"I told the voice I could no longer cope with the pain; after several years of depression and hopelessness I was unable to continue with my life. It told me … with as much love, empathy, and compassion that I could ever dream existed, that things were just not going to work that way. Basically, it said 'no.'"

"I asked if it could take away my depression. It replied, 'Yes, but if I were to take something from it, then I would have to give something in exchange.' It said that if I were to allow it to change my mental state, that it would be a permanent change and that I would not see things the same anymore. I would have a different view of relationships, a more realistic view of the world, of absolutely everything in life; my eyes would be opened to things I never saw before."

Anthony agreed to the trade-off. The presence then said, "It's done." But then there was nothing. He felt nothing—no change, no movement. There was nothing to indicate that anything had happened at all. He had the sensation, though, that the presence was gone as abruptly as it had appeared.

The voice had been silenced, and Anthony has never encountered the presence again.

"I then went to sleep and slept deeply for the first time in a long time," he recalled. "I wasn't drunk, I wasn't on drugs—I just went to sleep." And when he woke up the next morning something else was gone. "There was no depression, there was no fear, there was no dread about what was to come in my life. I was a new person." He was at first skeptical about the sudden change—about, as he put it, having depression turned off like a key turns off a car. He thought it would not last. He thought the depression would come back. "I went home. I got my daughter and began to really live my life. For months I expected those feelings to return. I didn't believe so much negative energy could just disappear in the blink of an eye. Every day I woke up surprised with the absence of pain."

He realized things that would have seemed self-evident to people who have not experienced depression. "My daughter is the most beautiful gift I have ever been given. How did I not see that?"

The encounter with the presence is the basis for who Anthony is today. He defines himself by the experience: "It was the true birth of the person I am." As for what it was he encountered in that threadbare room in Ban Thana, Anthony doesn't know and doesn't want to know; he has no intention of trying to figure it out. "I can guess at the origins of the presence. I sometimes believe it was my own subconscious acting out of self-preservation. I also am not much of a religious person but certainly don't discount the possibility of God or angels, and it could just as easily be explained that way. I have no idea, and I'm not searching for answers. I don't care about the truth of its origins because all that happened was that I became a functional human being who was capable of experiencing joy and happiness. Why does anything else matter?"

As Anthony explained it: "My experience was the best thing that has happened to me in my life. I have been forever changed and no longer experience depression or sadness in the ways that I used to. I have been 'given' all of the tools I need to experience a happy and fulfilling life. For this gift I am forever thankful to this being or third man."

"I was with what I felt and believe was the most intelligent, all-knowing, and powerful presence in all existence, and it brought absolute peace, love, and tranquility into a very turbulent life. It knew what I needed, and it gave it to me. It told me it gave it to me, and it took months for me to really believe that it was true."

He recalled a key moment in the conversation: "I asked the question that nobody really seems to ask … how can I be happy? It gave me happiness. At least, it didn't really give me happiness; it just removed the mental or emotional barriers to me being happy. It didn't really give me peace, either, but it showed me where I could find peace inside myself. I got other things I did not ask for or deem important at the time. It gave me compassion. It gave me objectivity. It gave me a sense of contentment that I had never known. I don't fear death; I believe I will have a 'companion' to go through that part of my life with, and I trust it completely. Everything is going to be okay. I just know that."

"I suppose I am just thankful to know that I am not alone."

Anthony was able to go from a state of terrible loneliness and intense pain and instead find an exhilarating sense of contentment and joy. By speaking with the presence, he had been able to alter the course of his life in ways that would have seemed previously unimaginable. The key was a recognition that he arrived at after a long difficult journey: that he was not alone.

PAULA RIDDLE'S SON was sixteen months old when she was diagnosed with inflammatory breast cancer in June 2003. It is a particularly aggressive form of breast cancer, and Paula was treated with a grueling regimen of chemotherapy, surgery, and radiation. She was then given a five-year course of Arimidex, an aromatase inhibitor. She finally finished taking the drug in June 2009, five years after her initial diagnosis. Symptom-free, she felt as if a dark cloud had finally lifted from her life and that of her family.

Then, six months later in the early daylight hours, Noah, Paula's husband, an accountant who had battled depression for years, parked his luxury car on the shoulder of a busy arterial roadway in Toronto, got out, walked to the edge of a bridge crossing a deep ravine, and jumped. It is impossible to know whether the stress and trauma surrounding her husband's death had any role in it, but six months after that, almost a year to the day after she had ended the Arimidex treatments, Paula learned that the cancer had returned. Her metastatic breast cancer had spread to her liver with innumerable metastases.

Within a week she was again undergoing chemotherapy, at the highest dose she could withstand, and was now taking the experimental drug Herceptin. At one point Paula overheard someone say that most people live twenty-two to twenty-six months with that kind of cancer, but she was not only fighting for herself; she had her young son to think about. In early May 2010 she had liver biopsies and a battery of other tests. She did one cycle of chemotherapy, but the following week her white blood cell count was too low, so she had to miss a week of chemotherapy. She took a drug to improve her white cell count, with the result that she ended up with too many white blood cells and was in considerable pain, but at least it allowed her to resume the chemotherapy.

Paula would be at the cancer hospital for ten-hour stretches. The type of chemotherapy she was undergoing did not make her nauseous, but she suffered terrible fatigue. She also felt like she was being scorched on the inside. Her skin actually looked as if she had spent too much time in the sun, and it became infected. She had scars up and down her arms. Sometimes it would take the nurse half an hour to find a vein to get the needle in.

When Paula returned home from her treatments she would crawl into bed and stay there. "I couldn't do anything," she remembered. "I couldn't even walk my son to school. I could barely turn on the light switch. I couldn't get my clothes out." She could not even read because she didn't have the ability to concentrate on anything. "I would just lay there with my eyes closed wishing for someone else's life," she said.

At one point Paula was so stressed that "I collapsed in the bathroom and my mother found me and said, 'Let's go to bed.' She didn't understand how much distress I was in. And my son came in and hugged me till I was breathing properly because I was hysterical. I calmed down, and my breathing became normal."

It was June. Paula had just undergone her third treatment and had returned home. She was lying in bed, covered in gray sheets and a duvet. Then there, next to the armoire, was Noah. "He was right beside it, standing there, telling me everything was going to be okay. I felt he was there. I felt it. It was very strong. When he died, he was gone. I never ever thought he would come back. I could feel he was gone. But at that moment he wasn't gone. He was there."

Paula closed her eyes for a few moments, and then looked again, and her husband was still there. "I remember seeing him there and hearing his voice, that distinctive rumble, saying everything was going to be okay and that I'd be fine and that he'd take care of me."

Her husband returned for several evenings in a row, usually for five or ten minutes, "when I was most tired." And then after another round of chemotherapy he returned again. "And over the course of a couple of weeks that kept happening," she said. On the last of the visits Paula began to speak to her husband. "It was a lot of uh-huhs. More of an awareness he was there trying to console someone who was inconsolable. And he wasn't good at it. That was never his strong suit, even when he was alive."

"I felt angry. I was angry I'd been sick. I was angry at my prognosis. Inflammatory breast cancer is a bad one to get. Recurrence is almost inevitable. I was furious that he killed himself, knowing it was likely I would get sick again. There is an inevitability to this illness. With the stress of his death, I was vulnerable to illness."

She was also angry that their son was without his father and had a mother who was now fighting for her life—that he could yet be left parentless. She raised this with Noah: "I talked to him about my anger over the way he died. I yelled at him. But I know I didn't yell at him aloud because my mother would have come running. It was a mental thing."

"I yelled at him in my head. I think it was a release. I shouted, and then he left."

She was surprised at herself, surprised that she had responded that way to his attempts to comfort her, and yet she was sure "the getting angry helped me get better. Statistically, there was a certain hopelessness to my situation. I am a medical freak. Getting angry forced me to want to stay with my son more and stay here more. It gave me a sense of relief, or chance to move on, or just to not die."

From that moment she has not seen Noah again. "I didn't need him. That was the day after the last CAT scan. The scan showed the cancer was getting smaller. And I started understanding I could go into a form of remission, a position where I have a fatal but manageable disease. That was a big deal."

Noah's appearance had not startled Paula, and she was equally not surprised that her husband had left her again. Of the experience, she said, "I accepted it. It didn't strike me as that weird. I knew he was there. I heard his voice. I communicated with him. I was convinced he was there." She is not at all religious and is uncertain what brought Noah to her bedside during the worst of her struggles: "I don't know. I never really worried about it. It was a small piece of grief."

In Paula's case, the presence of her dead husband had given her a chance to find closure. She had been at once sad and angry at him for choosing to leave her and their son, who she now had to raise alone, and she felt that his death had helped contribute in some way to her renewed fight with cancer. She was finally able to move beyond that and to begin to recover emotionally.

FOR MOST ADULTS the sensed presence is most likely to appear after a death. An astonishing proportion—some studies suggest it is as high as 50 percent—of those who are grieving will say they experience the presence of a deceased loved one. Sometimes they will report a visual or auditory encounter, but most frequently it is a "quasi-sensory, (partly) ineffable 'feeling' or a 'nonspecific awareness of presence'"—namely, they say they "somehow sense or feel the physical proximity of the deceased loved one."[8]

The examples range from a fleeting sense of a visit from the deceased to long conversations and, even in some more unusual cases, dinners with them, at least insofar as a place is set for the dead in the expectation that he or she will be dining. I call this the widow effect, because it was first identified as being prevalent among widows. However, it is widely reported among all people who suffer a loss: "post death contact is not a phenomenon restricted to a small segment of society such as widows and bereaved parents, but rather is an experience shared by numerous people who have experienced the death of many types of loved ones or close friends."[9] The result is that "adults are responding to stress in the same way children do ... by filling the void left by another."[10]

Until recently psychologists considered such cases as negative, even worrying evidence that an individual was "clinging on" to the deceased and refusing to face up to the reality of their loss.[11] In other words, it was not seen as helpful but rather as destructive and pathological, a sign of weakness or even mental illness. Such interpretations are hard to shake, with the result that many people who have had the experience would likely not want to admit to it. In fact, one researcher argued that a key factor that prevents people from disclosing what happened to them is a fear not of ridicule—though that is certainly also a factor—but that it could be "explained away." This is evidence that for some people at least, it is a deeply personal connection that needs to be protected. The 50 percent estimate may well be low.

Given how common these reports are, including across cultures, and the consoling effect they have, psychologists are now starting to look at them very differently. Study after study has concluded, in fact, that the experience is almost universally described as comforting and reassuring. It reduces loneliness, allows people to reestablish a sense of intimacy with the deceased as well as, in some cases, to resolve unfinished business with them. For parents who have lost children, the experience "has enabled them to maintain their identity as parents and has given them hope for a reunion with the deceased child."[12] Some psychologists have theorized that the sensed presence helps in the search for meaning in a death and can facilitate positive effects, contributing to what's been termed "posttraumatic growth."

Among the most interesting findings is the emerging evidence that people who can interpret their experience as having a spiritual basis "enjoy greater benefits as a result."[13] In fact, there are cases in which people describe feeling as if the deceased were a guardian angel. One study cites the case of a woman, who was quoted as saying, "I feel like my grandmother's been following me around and helping to protect me. Because I've done some pretty stupid things in my life and some of the things I should have almost died from, or should have died from and I didn't. So I feel like she's had a hand in that somehow. Either a voice or a force or something that, that pulled me away or said something at the last minute."[14] That study produced an astonishing finding: 53.5 percent of people surveyed reported feeling that the deceased are protecting them "or being a guardian angel."

CAROL WHITE was in her teens when her mother was diagnosed with breast cancer. Theirs was a religious family, and Carol believes the faith helped sustain her mother through a radical mastectomy and surgery to prevent the cancer from spreading. Her cancer then went into remission, but it was a short respite for the family, as the same cancer surfaced a few years later in Carol's eldest sister, Nancy, who had become like a second mother to Carol during their mother's serious illness.

Nancy was twenty-nine years old, very down to earth, and without airs. She had both breasts removed and was treated with radiation. But she still got ill. Carol spent a lot of time with her at the hospital. Nancy was remarkably stoic. She never complained. They drained her lungs, and Carol was there for that and held her hand, telling her, "'You can do this,' even though it was a difficult thing to sit through." And although Nancy was not prone to flights of fancy, when nothing worked and she was dying, she said someone would come to visit her. She told Carol it was her guide. "She would see him and sense him. He was waiting for her at the end of her life. She understood that he was trying to comfort her. It was a very powerful thing."

When Nancy died, Carol was grief stricken. She found her sister's loss to be such a hard one, especially on top of her mother's earlier illness. Nancy was an extrovert. She would talk to anyone. She had a ton of energy. She was always doing something. People who met her wouldn't forget her. She had a big impact on the people around her. It was hard to accept that she was gone, as her absence left a big hole.

Then a close friend of Carol's, Angela, was also diagnosed with breast cancer. Angela was very intelligent and gentle. As her condition deteriorated, she also said that she was experiencing visits. Already grieving one loss, Carol had to face another when her mother died. A sister, a mother, and a close friend, all dead in the space of a few years. It was a lot for anyone to cope with, a terrible burden of grief.

In the midst of this succession of traumas Carol was lying in bed one morning when suddenly she sensed someone else in her room. It was Nancy, and what's more, she had another person with her, a doctor. He was silent. Nancy said to Carol: "Don't worry, you won't get breast cancer. But you're having trouble in your lungs. You have to quit smoking."

The appearance of her sister did not startle or frighten Carol. "I felt so infinitely comforted by her presence. I was awake when this happened, and I was very sure it did happen. I felt flooded with comfort." Although the sense of loss was still acute, she then felt sure Nancy was still with her. "I was crying when it ended, but in a relieved way. I was so sure she was there. It had a huge impact on me, and the experience was never repeated. It altered my whole sense of life. It

⇒ 78 ⇐

gave me a sense of continuity, and I became even more certain after that, that there is life after death. I don't think this was a Catholic thing; it was more like a connection to her that couldn't be severed—she came to me."

From that day Carol never picked up another cigarette. She had previously tried to quit, but it had always proven too difficult, until Nancy's intervention. And then, two months later, Carol suffered a double bout of pneumonia. When she told her doctor that she had quit smoking two months earlier, he said that had likely saved her life. "I spent a long time, in fact, years afterwards thinking about this and trying to figure out what happened there. I had to grapple with the immense loss, but my terrible sense of desolation went away. It was like I got to see her again one more time after I had lost her and that she was still with me. It was definitely a benevolent presence. Nothing negative or frightening. The man who was there with her never said anything. Nancy was her old healthy self. She was glowing. I remember a light filled the room as she spoke to me. The vision lasted, I would say, about five minutes. It felt like I was in the presence of something holy. In fact, after this experience I went to talk to a nun to try to figure out what it meant. I remember the nun said to me: 'A family member can bring you to God.'"

And a sensed presence can bring comfort during a time of absence or loss.

Angela died soon after, but Carol went on living with a renewed sense of faith that we never truly lose the presence of those we love the most.

# - 4 -

# THE

# TAPLOW

# PEASANT

## HYPERSENSITIVE
## AGENT DETECTION
## DEVICE

VIDA ADAMOLI WAS MAKING HER WAY TOWARD THE train station in the picturesque English village of Taplow, Buckinghamshire. It was a beautiful afternoon in late September, and she was walking from Taplow Court, a large Victorian home now serving as a Buddhist center just outside the village, to Taplow Station. She was unstressed and thoroughly enjoying the country walk. She had spent a busy day meeting friends and proofreading a magazine, so she wasn't lonely or bored. The village, though idyllic, was deserted, and she was reflecting on how very different it would have been a century earlier, when it had been a thriving farming center rather than a bedroom community of London.

As Vida continued toward the station, a young man suddenly "materialized" in her path. It was more than the sense of a presence; she had an image of him: "He was wearing medieval, peasant-type clothes and resembled more a hologram than an actual person." At the time she was working hard to meet a book deadline, and her "imagination was easily stimulated and I often slipped into dreamy states of mind. I found myself wondering if the figure was a product of my imagination—and, if so, why had I come up with such a clichéd style of dress." She was not startled by the figure nor was she upset when he "seemed to 'melt' into me. I looked down and saw the young man's legs, with gaiters and crisscross shoe lacing, superimposed over my own."

The bizarre encounter confused her, but she was not shaken in any way, and when the impression had vanished, she continued on. But only moments later, as she was walking down a lane near the station, she "suddenly became aware of pounding footsteps behind me. I swung round just as a wild-eyed young man with disfiguring acne leapt on me and knocked me to the ground." It was a terrifying attack. "He lifted his foot to kick me in the face. I saw the huge boot with its patterned rubber sole bearing down—but it didn't hit me." In fact, the attacker tried several times to stomp on her. She was at risk of very serious injury, and yet "Each time I saw the boot coming at me, and each time it failed to make contact. It was as though it was prevented by an invisible barrier." Her assailant then grabbed her bag and ran off.

Once she had recovered from the shock of what had happened, Vida tried to understand it. In fact, it was very different from many sensed presence reports, which, for the most part, are experienced at the culmination of extreme stresses. In her case the translucent being had actually appeared before the attack, although the sense of protection remained with her throughout. "As someone living happily in a high-crime area of central London, the idea of being attacked in genteel Taplow would have seemed absurd. I am as mystified today as … when this incident happened."

Vida considered a number of possible explanations: "Was he a temporary embodiment of a protective force inherent in the universe—a 'guardian angel'? Or was he something conjured up by my brain? And, if so, what extraordinary ability does my brain possess that enables it to become aware of a random act of violence that will manifest sometime in the future? Whatever the answer, I believe the youth manifested minutes before I was attacked to save me from serious injury."

She attributed her protection to the vision of the peasant, feeling that it had some role in placing a protective "barrier" between herself and her attacker.

She reported the mugging and assault, and though police made inquiries, no one matching the description of the acne-pocked thug lived in the area. They concluded it was an opportunistic crime, telling her that the "young man was probably driving past when he spotted me walking alone down a deserted road." Understandably, she made no mention of the 'hologram' peasant to them.

Before she heard the pounding footsteps she had had no "intimation of danger," Vida said. But is it possible that she was, in fact, warned, that part of her brain was aware, subconsciously, of imminent danger?

ONE EXPLANATION of what happened on that September day in Taplow involves the activation of threat detection mechanisms within the temporal lobe, processes specialized for identifying cues for the presence of another. Psychologist Justin L. Barrett has named this internal vigilance system HADD—the hypersensitive agent detection device. Its function is to find and identify threats, and it is likely a vestige of our dangerous prehistory spent fending off animal predators and tribal enemies.

Here's how it works: after the alert that an agent was or is present is received, "human minds ... produce a wealth of inferences about the intentional states of the supposed agent," Barrett argued.[1] The potential for threat makes the agent's "beliefs, desires and intentions ... all immediately relevant matters." The process has what he termed, "significant implications for human survival." Correctly interpreting the readings can be a life-or-death matter.

The agency detection process is highly sensitive to even the slightest cue, from the rustling of leaves to a minute change in air currents in a room. As a result, it often produces false alarms. In many cases an explanation for the "movement, sound, trace" is quickly deduced, but in others no obvious explanation is found, Barrett says, and so "possible candidates for the agent and their various intentional states are immediately reviewed." Although some candidates, such as, say, a lion, are quickly ruled out "because of obvious circumstances, such as not being able to see them," that is not the case for others, which "because of their various counterintuitive properties, cannot be disconfirmed as explanations, thereby protecting their plausibility." Barrett goes on to caution that he is not arguing that "HADD experiences are directly responsible for belief in supernatural agents," but he does suggest that they can reinforce such beliefs.

In the case of Vida Adamoli, her internal alarm may have identified a possible threat. It need only have been some subtle movement, rustling, an awareness that a set of eyes were watching her, or a car slowing down in the distance—HADD identified something. At that moment this recognition entered her consciousness, except that in her "dreamy," creative mindset, she interpreted it not as a threat but as an externalized "hologram" that, bizarre as it was, she found oddly comforting, even empowering as it was absorbed into her being. It was only with the pounding of feet behind her did she register the true nature of the threat she was facing. Vida had a very real sense that an "invisible barrier," a sensation that is more difficult to explain, was protecting her. Was it her own instinctive defense that kept her from further harm?

IT WAS A GLORIOUS SUMMER MORNING, and Jodie Swales, an eighteen-year-old university student in Too-woomba, a city in south Queensland, Australia, decided to go to Queen's Park to study. She had a blanket with her to sit on, propped herself up against a large tree, and determinedly settled in to some reading before she planned to head to a class. At that time of day, not much past 7 A.M., no one else was in the park to disturb her, and she was lost in her studies. Then suddenly out of nowhere, a loud, clear voice said, "Watch out from behind the tree." She immediately turned around and saw that a man had been hiding behind the tree. When he realized she had seen him, he stepped forward and tried to make small talk. He looked very scruffy, with ill-fitting clothes, and he had stubble on his face. She did not feel afraid but did immediately think, "this guy is not right."[2] He asked her a few questions, including what she was read-ing. She felt the man was mentally ill, and "it was clear to me his intention was to attack me." She knew she had to get out of there quickly. Perhaps sensing this, he lunged for her, grabbed her, and tried to kiss her.

Jodie was prepared, however. The directive "watch out" had given her a fighting chance. As she put it: "I had certainly heard, very clearly, the message of an angel warning me."[3] But it was more than that; she had "an overwhelming sense that God, or Love, was by my side." In that respect she did feel a presence and was given a strength beyond that which she felt she possessed. She said it was like the sort of strength people discover at the scene of an accident where they have to lift up a car. Despite his grappling with her, she was able to slip free of the attacker, and though not physically strong, she was able to push him over and grab her books, blanket, and bag. She then ran to her car as the man ran away.

Later, Jodie read "studies that talk about people relying on something else as a coping mechanism, but in my experience I didn't even know the attacker was there, and I was told. I was warned about him by that audible voice at a crucial time. Had that voice warned me any later, I would have been attacked."[4] She felt she would have been unable to defend herself.

It's conceivable that HADD triggered a subconscious warning, that some cue below the threshold of her own awareness set off an alarm that was then brought to her attention in the form of an auditory hallucination. Of course, that fails to explain her ability to ward off the attack. Jodie has her own explanation for that. She believes an angel protected her. "I just feel so grateful to have heard that voice and to have been protected in the way I was. I'm starting to think that, that voice, whatever you want to call it, and I call it God, is always talking to me, but sometimes I'm not that great at listening."[5]

PSYCHOLOGIST J. ALLAN CHEYNE has suggested that the sense of presence "is the activation of a distinct and evolutionary functional 'sense of other' implicating structures deep within the temporal lobe specialized for the detection of cues for agency, especially those potentially associated with threat or safety." According to Cheyne's theory, "the feeling itself is simply a dissociation of the normal feeling of the presence of others associated with the normal cues for their physical presence."[6]

The sense of the presence of others is pervasive, Cheyne argued, and usually exists continuously at the background level in the manner of elevator music. We obviously experience it when we actually *are* with other people. In order to experience it, there is a simple test: if you are in a room with a friend, ask her to remain motionless and silent, and then close your eyes, "the other's presence is still clearly felt, even despite the absence of visual, auditory or tactile signs."[7] The psychologist Tore Nielsen suggested that the sensation that "someone is there ... is an integral part of our everyday experience." For the most part we think nothing of it and, indeed, are unaware of it. At other times, however, it does register. "We feel it explicitly when in intense relationships and acutely when in love," Cheyne noted, "but mostly it is just the reassuring background feeling of companionship. Our feeling corresponds with recent memory and with current sensory experience."[8]

It is when that feeling disconnects from explicit perceptual cues of others that "the [disembodied] sensed presence" can be generated.[9] In one of his papers Cheyne noted that "agency detection devices come especially to the fore in emergency situations, in which thresholds are lowered and agency detection bias is increased."[10] It is more than just a misfiring of the agency detection mechanism, a false alarm; it actually plays a constructive role and so could itself be a survival adaptation, although Cheyne did not go so far as to argue that. Still, he did point out what so many cases illustrate: when a person is facing high levels of stress, the need for companionship "activates the feeling of presence." This serves as a comfort to people in need and "could be construed as incidentally functional."[11]

It can be more than just an alarm, however. Both Vida Adamoli and Jodie Swales felt as though the presence continued to protect them as they were being attacked. Kelly Smith was in a very different situation, where the alarm, when it sounded, was too late to help. She was trapped, but still she found help.

IT WAS FRIDAY NIGHT in a small town in California, at the start of the Labor Day weekend in 1980. Kelly Smith, a slim, attractive, twenty-two-year-old woman, was headed for a country-and-western nightclub four miles away in the neighboring town to meet her boyfriend. She called to tell him that her car had broken down earlier that day and that she was going to take a bus up to the club. He offered to come pick her up, but she told him not to bother; he owned the bar, and it was busy at the time. She said she would be there soon. Kelly walked to a bus stop near a busy crossroads, just as it was starting to rain. At first it spat a few drops. Then the sky opened, and there was no bus in sight. Impulsively, Kelly stuck her thumb out, hoping someone would take pity on her. Moments later a small truck pulled up. The driver, a burly man in his late twenties with wire-rimmed glasses, straw-colored hair, and a pockmarked face, leaned over and opened the passenger door. He smiled as she jumped in and told him where she was headed. He said he was going in the same direction and would be happy to drop her.

The man introduced himself, and there was a monogrammed necklace hanging from his rearview mirror, with his name in script style. He admitted to Kelly that he had been drinking at a holiday party, although she could detect no smell of alcohol. He was playing Supertramp, which at the time was her favorite band, and she was relaxed. Then the man turned off the main street they had been on and headed down a dark road. Kelly grew worried but then wondered if she had any reason to be. She thought that it might be a shortcut, as the road they were on also led to where they were going. "Oh, you are going to take the back way to the club?" she asked. "Yes," he replied. She was a little nervous now, and her guard was up.

Then he made a sudden right, instead of a left, which would have taken them in the direction of the club. At that point she got upset and tried to open the door to jump out. There was a police car coming toward them as the truck headed into an industrial area. He grabbed her with one hand and threatened her: "If you jump out, I will kill you." The cruiser had passed. He turned into a parking lot and pulled in front of a dumpster. Kelly was now very frightened. The man pulled a buck knife and ordered her to climb through a small window that led to the camper shell that covered the back of the truck. She followed his instructions. There was a rope and a milk crate in the back. The man got out, walked around, and crawled in. He sat on the milk crate and ordered Kelly to take her clothes off. He had the huge knife in his hand. After she disrobed, he then forced her to perform oral sex on him as he held the knife to her throat. Kelly knew that after the sexual abuse, his intention was to kill her and put her body in that dumpster.

That's when she became aware of a presence behind her, and it was powerful. "It was taller than the truck and immensely, incredibly strong," Kelly recalled. A voice told her that her life was in peril and that she must follow its commands. She spoke to her assailant, but the words were not her own. "Words fell out of my mouth right after that. I said to him, 'If you kill me, my five-year-old daughter will grow up without a mother.' Those were the words this 'Being' put in my mouth. I felt strength, and words came to me from this 'deliverer.'"

Kelly looked into her attacker's face and could see a change come over it. "You could see his eyes unglaze as he shook his head." He then said, "Oh no, not again." He stared at Kelly and said at last, "Oh my God, I am so sorry." He instructed her to get dressed and crawl back into the front seat. He stepped out and then came around the truck and got back into the driver's seat. Kelly had a sense of strength and continued to speak but felt none of the words were really her own. "I totally felt a presence, like a strong being who was with me, flowing his strength into my heart." She demanded that the man hand over the knife, which amazingly he did. He then asked her to place it into the glove compartment, which she did.

They sat for a long time. She was hoping that he would let her go and was reasoning with him and counseling him. She was still in great danger, and at one point he seemed to "snap" and lurched at the knife. But Kelly commanded him to return it and remained very much in control. He did return the knife and never laid another hand on her. Kelly attributed this to a barrier that she felt had physically separated them. She said it was as if the presence had embraced her, making it impossible for the man to renew his attack. "I thought I was crazy for thinking that, but looking back, there was probably a spiritual barrier between us."

He finally took Kelly to the club, and she called the police and filed a report with a description of the man, but he was never found. In all, her ordeal had lasted over three hours, but she was alive and to this day is convinced that all that stood between her and certain death was the presence, a force that intervened at a critical moment and made it possible for her to talk her assailant out of murder.

TAKING HER LUNCH BREAK, twenty-year-old Liz Gregori was sauntering down Wiltshire Boulevard on a warm March day in Los Angeles, California, when she walked into the middle of a bank heist. Bullets were actually flying, and she was right in the line of fire, frozen with terror.

Two young men had tried to rob the bank, but police were alerted and had arrived before they could get away. The robbers grabbed hostages and moved toward their car, just as Liz arrived outside the bank. The men and the hostages jumped into a small car, with the rear window glass blown out at the back. One of the men leveled his shotgun at her. She locked eyes with him.

Just then she felt a presence materialize immediately beside her, and she began to read the situation in a much more detailed way that she ought to have. She was being fed details, not only about what to do herself but how the situation was going to unfold: "The angel told me to stand exactly where I was and not to move." Every instinct made her want to run for cover. "I wanted to bolt. ... It was the natural thing to do, to move—run." But she heeded the instructions, received mentally, from the presence, which she felt was male. "I did as the angel said."

She was calm and followed the instructions because she "knew absolutely … appearances notwithstanding, I would not be the one to die that day, no matter how the distribution of power looked at that moment. I knew that he would die, and I felt sorry for him.

"I still remember his face." He looked as if he were considering whether or not to fire, but she then felt as if a veil came between them: "He didn't seem to see me anymore. He turned his attention away and was dead within minutes."

Then, just as abruptly, she felt the presence leave. "My angel was gone the second I was out of danger." She was struck that no one around her was aware of the awesome power that had intervened. Not only was she protected, but she also had a greater awareness that seemed to take in the fates of others. It was a level of insight that is hard reconcile with neurological processes alone, such as HADD. The gunfire had left the two robbers dead, along with two hostages.

# - 5 -

# THE

# INTERPRETER

## RIGHT-HEMISPHERIC
## INTRUSIONS

WHEN MELISSA FOX-REVETT'S FIRST CHILD, LINDSAY, was born in a Toronto hospital, she was thrilled with the result, but the whole experience of giving birth disappointed her profoundly. "I was flat on my back, wired to machines, denied food, induced for a doctor's convenience, and stoned out of my mind on medications which I know were intended to relieve pain but I suspect had the happy side-effect of making me compliant and complicit," Melissa recalls. She determined then and there that her next delivery would be an altogether different experience. It would be at home, with the help of a midwife.

When she was in the last stage of her second pregnancy, her water broke, appropriately enough, on Labour Day. Her son, Cameron, however, did not arrive until four days later, very early on a Thursday morning. Melissa spent the intervening days close to home, wondering when her child would finally see fit to emerge. If a doctor rather than a midwife had attended her, she knew that she would most likely have been rushed to the hospital and induced in short order. But her midwife told her that she could wait for nature to take its course.

When Cameron at last made his imminent arrival known, Melissa felt pressure and a sporadic but intensifying pain. That night she ate dinner with her husband, shared a little wine, put her daughter to bed, and settled in to watch a film. Her husband would pause the video every time a contraction hit, resuming the film only when it subsided. They didn't get to finish the movie; Melissa reached the point when she could no longer concentrate on anything other than what was happening inside of her.

She called the midwife, her sister, and a friend, all of whom rushed over. She was at the center of a swirl of activity as the bed was prepared, towels laid out, and lights were dimmed, as the midwife unpacked all the paraphernalia for a home birth.

It was now late at night and dark outside. The windows were open. Melissa was completely engaged by the pain that escalated in waves of bone-searing agony. "During each contraction it felt as if my spine was being ground down from the inside," she said. It was very difficult for her to breathe. She knelt at the side of her bed. To an observer, it might have looked as though she were at prayer, except that Melissa has never been religious. The pain was excruciating; the anticipation of each wave, gathering in intensity, was nearly as hard for Melissa to endure as the pain itself.

The only way she could cope was to completely shut out everything around her. She lost all sense of time. She heard no voices, saw no lights, and was aware of no movement around her. She didn't speak except to ask that no one touch or talk to her. At one point she heard a bear-like bellow, looked around, and then asked, "Is that me? Did I make that sound?"

At that moment she felt a sense of detachment, as though she were looking down from the ceiling at herself. But then the experience grew in intensity, and she realized there was another being present, looking over her right shoulder. And that being was communicating with her mentally.

"The person over my shoulder was not me," she said. "It was encouraging me, telling me how wonderful I was—that I was strong and powerful." She found the experience awe inspiring, and from that moment on felt no further pain. "I did feel strong and powerful. I did feel like a bear."

Melissa is unsure whether her experience with the presence lasted minutes or hours, just that it ended abruptly with Cameron's birth at 4:33 A.M. Even so, the presence left that feeling of power with her. She felt no pain after the birth, and for the next few hours experienced tremendous energy and euphoria. "It was the most profoundly spiritual and deeply moving episode of my entire life," Melissa would recall.

MANY OF THOSE who experience a sensed presence will offer, without prompting, that the being was on their right side, usually over their right shoulder. This happens time and again. It happened to Melissa, and it happened to me. At least five of the explorers and climbers I included in *The Third Man Factor* also said that the presence was to their right. Here's how the climber Reinhold Messner described it in his book, *The Naked Mountain*: "Suddenly there was a third climber next to me. He was descending with us, keeping a regular distance a little to my right and a few steps away from me, just out of my field of vision. I could not see the figure and still maintain my concentration, but I was certain there was someone there. I could sense his presence; I needed no proof." By contrast, there are reports of a presence being located on a person's left, but they are unusual in comparison.

This raises the intriguing possibility that under stress, the normally dominant left cortical hemisphere starts to lose its grip. In our study Peter Suedfeld and I suggested that this in turn reduces "the preponderance of logical, linear, reality-oriented thinking. The right hemisphere, which, to put it simplistically, governs creative, imaginative, nonlinear cognition, assumes a greater role than usual; and its products, which may include the perception of an imagined 'other,' enter consciousness."[1] A variation on this idea was advanced by researcher Todd Murphy, who has suggested the sensed presence surfaces when "the right hemispheric sense of self falls out of phase with the left hemispheric self."[2] There is also the intriguing possibility that the sensed presence may be the product of what neuroscientist Michael Gazzaniga has termed "the Interpreter."

Most of the specialist systems built into our brains work automatically and outside of conscious awareness and control. A person can be exposed to some stimuli fleetingly or opaquely, without it entering consciousness at all. Yet these automatic processes may still have registered stimuli and responded.[3] That changes, however, when the Interpreter gets involved. According to Gazzaniga, once the brain takes in an event, "there is a special device in the left brain, which I call the Interpreter, that carries out one more activity upon completion of zillions of automatic brain processes. The Interpreter, the last device in the information chain in our brain, reconstructs the brain events."[4] It is, he says, the brain's storyteller, collecting inputs and making sense of them in the grand scheme of things. It is why we experience unified consciousness. We are quite literally of one mind. He says the Interpreter also creates the impression that our brain is working at our behest, and "not the other way around."

Support for the existence of the Interpreter was demonstrated in patients who had their corpus callosum, the major connection between the two hemispheres, cut to prevent the spread of epileptic seizures. Gazzaniga experimented by sharing instructions only with the right hemisphere of several patients, and in each case the left-hemisphere Interpreter made up stories to explain their resulting actions. In one case he showed the word "walk," and the patient did as instructed and started walking. The left brain, which was unaware of the instruction, was at a loss for an explanation, yet the Interpreter cooked one up anyway. When asked why he was walking, the patient said, "I wanted to go get a Coke."[5] Such explanations are offered as absolute truths, even when they are transparently—even sometimes comically—false.

Neurologists believe the sense of self is housed in the left hemisphere. If people have the sense that an unseen companion is on their right side, because the "left and right brain circuits are criss-crossed so that, for example, the right visual field is registered in the left hemisphere's visual cortex," then, as Michael Shermer argued, "The sensed presence may be the left-hemisphere interpreter's explanation for right-hemisphere anomalies."[6]

SUSAN DENIS WAS IN THE MIDDLE of a momentous change. For several years she operated a flourishing bed and breakfast, Eastport House, in Annapolis, Maryland. The historic residence sat near the harbor and became a favorite for visitors to Annapolis. But in June 2012 Susan was in the midst of moving. She had sold the house, and her life was "in a pod." She and her partner, David, were moving to North Carolina. It was June 16, just a few days before the deal's closing, when she began to feel a little lightheaded. At first she attributed it to the stress of the move. Then the symptoms became more ominous: she found she couldn't remember words. Still, she had no sense of urgency but nonetheless made an appointment to see her physician and hopped on her Segway for the short journey. After a consultation she was told she could not Segway home but instead had to be driven.

Barely a week later Susan had CT and MRI scans at Johns Hopkins in Baltimore. The diagnosis was serious: a rare and often terminal form of cancer. Surgeons operated on June 27 and removed a tumor from the temporal region of her brain. Her sister was in the waiting room, and David planned to arrive at noon to spend the afternoon. "My sister says the doctor told her I would sleep that afternoon, so she called David and insisted he not come to visit." Instead, her sister went sailing that afternoon, having told several of Susan's friends: "I was to have no visitors, as she thought quiet would be good for me."[7] The result was that when she awoke in her room in the intensive care unit, she discovered that no one was there to see her. She had no visitors at all. The only person there was a nurse, who came in and out. She felt bereft of companionship, and, confronting her own mortality, she needed support. For Susan their absence was a mystery that left her feeling intensely alone. She could not move her head as a result of the surgery. Her sense of isolation was compounded by the absence of her prescription glasses, which had been removed for the surgery.

Then that evening, she became aware of having some visitors, but it was not anyone she had expected. "I was laying there, thinking about other things, then felt something important was around, and then I knew it was them." It was her mother, Margaret, her grandmother Elsie, and her "pretend little brother," a young man named Ty, all of whom were dead. "I was so pleasantly surprised they were there visiting me. I had a sense of them there. It wasn't until after a few hours that they left."

With their arrival Susan then sat back and relaxed. "It changed everything," she said. "I heard them, they talked to me, especially [saying] don't worry about where I'd be going—it would be to join them." The three were to Susan's right in the room. She could not and did not see them: "Their message was, 'We're here to let you know you're close to us, don't be afraid, we're here.'" She heard the words clearly, although it was a "mental communication."[8] Their presence was a great comfort to her as she lay there alone, recovering from surgery and confronting an uncertain future. "After they departed, tears joyfully rolled down my cheeks, and I have been at peace about this illness, even a week later, when I was told the results were terminal." Nearly a year later Susan is in remission, but her encounter continues to console her. "It was very helpful, and it is still a comfort. I feel that God, or Jesus gave me them to help me. I've always believed in God—to me it's straightforward. Now I have no question."

Angele Blais was nursing her first child, an infant daughter, when the telephone rang. It was her former husband, Michel. A maid answered the phone and told Angele who was on the line. Even though she had remarried, she still spoke with Michel from time to time and normally would have taken the call; however, she made a practice of not talking on the phone when she was nursing. "I said I couldn't speak to him and ask him to leave a message." The maid said later that Michel had called from Guatemala. Had she known that at the time, Angele said, she would have spoken to him.

Two days later she received a call from Michel's sister, who said her former husband was dead. He had suffered a heart attack in Guatemala. "It is impossible," replied Angele. "He cannot be dead. He was calling me two days ago." The sister said that's when he had died, two days earlier. The time of death coincided with the time of his call. "It was exactly when he called emergency." Michel was dying when he made the call. The young man, who was only twenty-seven at the time of his death, had been struggling with a drug problem. This was the reason they had broken up, although he had initiated the split. Angele was distraught over the thought that she had failed to speak to him and wondered what he would have said or if she could have helped in some way. "I felt very disappointed that I did not take that call. It did bother me tremendously."

Further contact with his family made it clear that she would not be welcome at his funeral: "I was banned. They must have felt I was responsible."

A day or two later Angele was again nursing at her home in Sorel, Quebec, when she suddenly felt the presence of Michel with her, immediately at her right side. "He was there, always beside me on my right side, a presence that was not threatening but consoling. It was bigger than life, and I did not see him, as in, I did not look right into his eyes, but he was there physically. I saw him out of the corner of my eye."

"He was more present and real to me than any other thing, even things I could touch."[9]

Again, the left brain seems to recognize the presence in this case in extracorporeal space to the right. Perhaps the more imaginative brain becomes predominant, and the Interpreter reads its products as a distinct being.

Angele said it was a very reassuring and calm experience. "It was comforting. I felt as if I almost did not exist, that it was him more than me. He was there, part of me." The sense of Michel's presence lasted for a full week, he moved when she moved, he stood when she stood. "He was there constantly for a week, when I went to bed, and when I woke up." She told her second husband, Jocelyn, "I am sleeping with a ghost. He is with me right now. I could not believe it myself." Then after a week she knew Michel was gone. It happened as abruptly as it had begun. "He was no longer there. I felt a little bit lost."

When Michel was with her, Angele had felt no need to talk, but afterward she wanted him desperately to return, but he never did. "I remember trying to reproduce that feeling many times afterwards but it was impossible." She felt that she had missed her opportunity. "I had my chance and did not take it, I suppose." Twice she had that chance, when he had telephoned her and when his presence had visited her and comforted her, and twice she did not communicate. She wondered then and wonders to this day what the purpose of both experiences was, what it was he had wanted to tell her. Even so, she had felt better at the end; the presence had allowed her to let go of the disappointment and guilt she had felt and to return to raising her young child.

WHEN IN HIS TWENTIES, living alone on Beacon Hill in Boston, the psychologist Julian Jaynes was grappling with some particularly complex ideas that would eventually form the basis for his utterly original and also controversial theory of the bicameral mind. He was feeling great stress. At one point he lay down on a couch in a state of, as he put it, "intellectual despair." Abruptly, a "distinct loud voice from my upper right" broke the silence. The voice not only provided him with a clue that formed the basis for his theory, but it was also so real that it startled him. "It lugged me to my feet absurdly exclaiming, 'Hello?' looking for whoever was in the room. The voice had had an exact location. No one was there! Not even behind the wall where I sheepishly looked." Jaynes did not consider the command to have been "divinely inspired, but I do think that it is similar to what was heard by those who have in the past claimed such."[10]

Jaynes called his theory bicameralism and argued that consciousness is a late development in human evolution. As recently as a few thousand years ago, at the first light of history, humans existed in a preconscious state, and experienced the products of their right cortical hemisphere as real-life external events: "Images and ideas generated by that hemisphere were interpreted as a presence and communication of a god or some other entity."[11] What is more, the slightest stress, even making a simple decision, such as where to hunt, could be enough to elicit the voices.

It was a more ancient form of decision making, in which the decisions were left to a greater power, in the form of internal prompts, brain commands by way of authoritative voices—a "repeated 'internal' verbal hallucination telling him what to do."[12] Today, when confronted with events, "we quickly and efficiently swivel our consciousness over to the matter and narratize out what to do," said Jaynes. Our bicameral antecedents, however, would have to wait for nonconscious directions. Such voices were real to those who heard them, just as real as the voice Jaynes himself had heard. "It is absolutely certain that such voices do exist and that experiencing them is just like hearing actual sound," he said.

Further, he considered imaginary companions in childhood "another vestige of the bicameral mind." He noted that they generally occur before age seven, preceding what he regarded as the full development of consciousness in children. He also raised the possibility that children who experienced an imaginary companion might be more susceptible to encountering a presence later in life.

Literacy, which introduced another way to relay the commands of God, helped to break down the bicameral mind and usher in unified consciousness, "as linear thinking led us to perceive the process of both hemispheres as fully belonging to the person, not to outside sources."[13] Yet, Jaynes added, today many normal people still hear such voices, often during times of stress. Essentially, the sensed presence fits neatly into the theory of bicameralism, as a vestigial remnant, in which stress reawakens a very different kind of brain for those who experience it: a more ancient brain. It is an evocative idea, and it is the only nonreligious theory that has anything to say about the "dramatic helpfulness" of the sensed presence.

Whether it is the Interpreter or reversion to a bicameral mind or some other explanation, what is clear is that the presence, or angel, usually appears to a person's right, which could be significant in terms of an organic explanation for the phenomenon. But then again, there is always a spiritual counterargument. God exalted Jesus above all others by seating Him at the right hand of the Father.

# TOBY

# THE

# SWIMMER

## EXECUTIVE FUNCTION
## VERSUS
## LOW-ROAD EMOTION

THE CRASH OF AIR FRANCE FLIGHT 447 COULD HAVE been averted. That was the conclusion of French investigators in their final report on the air disaster. They described a "profound loss of understanding" by three experienced pilots after alarms sounded when the aircraft entered a major storm system, ice crystals threw off the plane's sensors, and the autopilot disconnected. The Airbus A330–200 crashed over the Atlantic Ocean on June 1, 2009, killing all 216 passengers and 12 aircrew while on a scheduled flight from Rio de Janeiro to Paris. One theory is that the pilots' inability to mentally function in a state of panic caused the crash: "Under pressure, human beings can lose their ability to think clearly and to properly execute their training."[1]

Flight-data recorders recovered after the disaster recorded one of the copilots telling the captain, who had taken a break just before the crisis and rushed back into the cockpit: "We totally lost control of the plane. We don't understand it at all. We've tried everything." In his analysis of the crash, Jeff Wise, who has made a study of the organic basis for fear, explained, "Psychologists who study performance under pressure are well aware of the phenomena of 'brain-freeze,' the inability of the human mind to engage in complex reasoning in the grip of intense fear." Wise states that in the face of a rapidly accelerating calamity, the pilots could not figure out what was happening to the aircraft: "Despite numerous boldfaced clues to the nature of their problem—including a stall warning alarm that blared 75 times—they were simply baffled."[2]

Panic seemed to shut down the pilots' thinking. Fear centers of the brain do not allow for problem solving but instead fall back on a series of instinctive responses. The Air France pilots were unable to recognize even their simplest problem, which turned out to be that one of them had the stick pulled back the whole time, causing the plane to climb into an aerodynamic stall. Their thinking—their capacity to reason—was closing off, leaving only "instinctive behavior."

One theory for the sensed presence is that it is a by-product of such a process, activated by extreme stress. In such a situation conflict arises between the brain's executive function—controlled cognitive processes like reasoning or decision making that people knowingly employ—and automatic emotions that function unconsciously, below the radar, as it were, such as trembling or blanching, a surge of hormones, and emotional associations with past unpleasantries that trigger unconscious actions. In such situations these controlled and automatic brain systems start to vie for supremacy. As the threat intensifies, the body begins to switch off higher functions, leaving the field open for basic survival responses. As Michael Shermer wrote in *The Believing Brain*: "At high levels of stimulation (as in extreme environmental conditions and physical and mental exhaustion), low-road emotions can so overrun high-road cognitive processes that people can no longer reason their way to a decision; they report feeling 'out of control' or 'acting against their own self-interest.' Perhaps this is when the brain calls forth the sensed presence companion."[3]

Absent executive control—and, so, absent coordinated, purposeful behavior—emotions run amok, thus, Shermer suggested, "enabling inner voices and imaginary companions to arise."[4] It is sort of a neurological manifestation of the old adage, "When the cat's away, the mice will play." Only, in this case, the mice are not getting into the pantry, chewing through wires or nesting in the linen, nor are they out of control; in fact, it would have been better had the Air France pilots let the mice in.

If the sensed presence is the product of a conflict in the brain in which "low-road" emotions are triumphant, then you would not expect to encounter what the French pilots were experiencing. To the contrary, instead of brain freeze and the resulting chaos and mass death, something extraordinary could have happened. A presence could have instilled a sense of calm, encouragement, and clarity. It might have issued commands that would have assisted them through their predicament, possibly even presenting them with a solution, as simple as "push forward on the control stick." It may well have seen them through their crisis.

That's what happened to another pilot, Brian H. Shoemaker, after his helicopter lost radio contact in Antarctica. Shoemaker had piloted a group of scientists through the Trans-Antarctic Mountains to the Antarctic Plateau. He was on the return journey in the H-34 helicopter when he effectively found himself flying blind. Without radio contact with McMurdo Station and with no navigator, he and his copilot could not get a fix on their position. He could not see the mountains or other landmarks since the landscape was essentially white and featureless from the air. He worried that he was flying in circles and also that there was a real danger that he would use up the helicopter's fuel supply before ever reaching his destination.

It was not an acute crisis like what the Air France pilots had faced, but it was a crisis all the same, and with the danger increasing by the minute and his sense of anxiety mounting, Shoemaker suddenly felt a "guiding presence" standing immediately behind him. It spoke to him, assuring him: "You're doing alright."[5] The presence then began to issue very specific instructions. If he heeded them, he would survive. At one point it said, "Turn to a heading about 20 degrees to the right." He turned the H-34 to the precise heading the presence had commanded, although said nothing to his copilot. "I had nothing else to go by. ... It was eerie. It wasn't frightening. It was a solace. That was the decision I had to make; follow it, or follow my own, and I had no idea which way to go." Instead of brain freeze, he consciously followed the presence's advice. The presence remained for at least half an hour, as the helicopter found the mountains and Shoemaker established his correct route in to McMurdo. Only then did the guiding presence leave.

So what was happening to Brian Shoemaker? Possibly, his brain, on autopilot of some sort because of the stress, was picking up cues that he was consciously missing, cues that flew under the radar of his higher executive functions, and then transmitted them to him in the form of commands from an unseen being, a presence that offered him a way out. Or perhaps it was something more.

THREE HOURS AFTER it took off from Gander, Newfoundland, on September 23, 1962, a Flying Tiger Line Lockheed Constellation, en route on a military charter from McGuire Air Force Base, New Jersey, to Frankfurt, Germany, had a fire in one of the aircraft's four engines. The engine was shut down and its propeller feathered. A few minutes later a second propeller oversped when the flight engineer inadvertently closed a firewall shutoff valve. This engine also had to be shut down. Efforts to restart the engine failed. Captain John D. Murray calculated that the flight was eight minutes past the Equal Time Point between North America and Europe. Gander Air Traffic Control asked FT 923 if it was returning to Gander, Newfoundland, but the flight crew replied "proceeding to Shannon," in Ireland.

An hour later a third engine developed serious problems and a fire warning sounded. The sixty-eight passengers were asked to don their lifejackets. The engine fire warning again sounded, so power was reduced and the warning stopped. A short time later the engine failed. With only one engine working, Murray turned on the public address system and said, "Ladies and gentlemen, this is the captain speaking. We are going to ditch."[6] Passengers were advised to take their shoes off; remove and stow any dentures, pens, pencils, glasses, jewelry, and sharp objects; put a blanket and pillow on their legs; and clasp their hands and arms around their legs. The crew also put on their lifejackets.

Some passengers were assigned tasks, such as opening emergency exits when the time came. Two soldiers were asked to remove the emergency life raft from the crew compartment and place and secure it near the rear main exit door. Other soldiers were assigned to, after they ditched, deploy life rafts stored externally from the wings. A number of the soldiers treated the crisis with bravado and high spirits, even telling one of the flight attendants they'd like her to join them in their life raft.

The cabin lights were dimmed so those aboard could become accustomed to the darkness. As the Flying Tiger descended toward the Atlantic, passengers shared their last thoughts and moments together. Major Richard Elander said to his wife, Lois: "Thank you, darling, for a wonderful nine years." She replied, "Sweetie, it's been a wonderful life. I am glad I knew you."[7] Flashlights were not mandatory equipment, and what few were located on the aircraft were distributed to key people. At the last moment the captain pulled the nose of FT 923 up. Five minutes after the captain's announcement, the aircraft made contact with the water. There were no skips or subsequent impacts.

The deceleration after hitting the water was severe. One of the aircraft's wings was torn off. The captain's head struck the instrument panel, opening a gash on his forehead. He had trouble seeing because of the profuse bleeding but nonetheless grabbed a flashlight and left the cockpit. In the passenger compartment some of the seats had broken loose and had gotten tossed around the cabin. The emergency exits were opened and the life raft deployed on the left side of the plane. Water began to pour into the cabin as passengers and the eight crew scrambled to exit.

The last person known to have exited the plane later told investigators that he believed no one was left on board the plane, although interior damage caused by the severe impact may have concealed some victims.

The water was rough, covered with whitecaps, with waves reaching twenty feet. Passengers swam or treaded water, some crying out "Help!" and screaming, as others shouted, "Where are the rafts? Where are the boats?" In the end only one life raft was successfully deployed. Some people found it with the help of the flashlight the captain held. Even then, their survival was in doubt. The raft was crowded, and people were hanging from the sides. When some of them tried to clamber aboard, someone shouted, "It's too crowded!"[8]

One survivor said he saw a woman swim to the side. "I tried to pull her aboard but men poured over us like sardines. I held on and she kept crying, 'Please let me up.' But they kept on coming over and around us. I found myself under a pile of men and I could not hold on. The woman disappeared."[9]

Passenger Art Gilbreth experienced a mysterious intervention that helped him to survive. He had suffered crushed vertebrates after the seat he was belted to dislodged at impact, and he and the seat had been thrown through the cabin. In fact, all the seats on the right side of the cabin, from the over-the-wing emergency exit to the last row, failed. "As a result of the pileup of these seats, some passengers experienced considerable difficulty in extricating themselves."[10]

Gilbreth was initially unable to free himself and was only able to escape when the water reached his neck. He couldn't see anything, and the aircraft was quiet save for the sound of the rushing water. He followed a line of white water that proved to be water pouring into the aircraft, denoting the exit. Once outside, he encountered a woman who cried out, "Help me, I can't swim." He was able to find the cord on her life vest and it inflated. She thanked him, but a large wave hit and separated them. He looked for her, but she was gone.

Gilbreth saw the raft and began to swim toward it. He noticed a large object to his right and thought at first it was a shark, then recognized the tail fin of the Constellation. He realized he was swimming over the fuselage of the submerged aircraft. One of the fins then caught his right leg and he was pushed underwater, into the cold, dark North Atlantic. He then experienced the sensation that there was another being nearby, hovering, he thought, above him. "The voice kept telling me to kick the silver thing below me. It kept saying 'harder, harder!'"[11]

The silver object was the tail fin of the aircraft, and it slipped further underwater. "Then I realized I was underwater and did not know which way was up. The voice told me to relax and I did. I could feel the water passing down my cheek and realized the surface was above me. I started swimming as hard as I could. During all this time I had not felt like I was running out of breath nor did I feel pain, but as soon as I broke surface I took the biggest loudest breath I have ever taken." He then saw a light on the raft and swam toward it, and was saved.

A mysterious helper also saved Carmen Figueroa, of San Juan, Puerto Rico. Carmen too had been forced to jump into the wild ocean at night. She was traveling with her husband. Separated, she found high waves and wind moved her away from the sinking aircraft, into a void of darkness. She was completely disoriented and alone. Then, out of nowhere, a young man emerged from the darkness, and was swimming toward Carmen. He called to her confidently: "Follow me, swim this way!"

Carman asked, "Where is the raft?!" The young man answered in a "commanding voice," "The raft is this way, follow me." She was puzzled and asked, "How do you know?" He replied loudly, "Trust me, follow me. I know." Carman swam after him into pitch darkness. She could not see or hear anything to indicate a raft was nearby. After swimming for a few minutes through the inky seas, she started to hear voices, "people crying and yelling," and then saw the raft. She swam toward it, and as she reached the crowded raft, before she was pulled aboard, she asked her guide, the young man:

"What is your name?" "They call me Toby," he replied. She thanked him as he swam off, possibly, she thought, to aid others.

In all, fifty-one people reached the life raft and boarded it, exceeding its capacity by more than 100 percent. People were crammed to the edges, which began to take on water over the sides, and the survivors had to bail continuously, using a cap and plastic bags. The wind and sea pounded the raft. At times the raft was spun around, and at others it would rise high on the crest of a wave, only to be dropped. Sometimes, the raft was caught between two waves and folded together, forcing the passengers even more tightly together. There were cries of pain. Some survivors had to hold the heads of others out of the water. "The raft was filling with water," one survivor, Fred Caruso, recalled. "Waves would wash in. We were submerged in icy water from the chest down. It was so cold. The water so rough. We bobbed around like a cork."[12]

Aircraft could be heard overhead, which kept people's hopes up. Occasionally someone would think they saw a light on the horizon and would yell, "A ship is coming!" Even the rising moon was mistaken for a ship, but the excitement would soon die down as people discovered the error. After four hours, however, a searchlight could be seen in the distance, and from the top of waves the light could be glimpsed, slowly growing closer.

Some of those on the raft had been injured; others suffered from shock and exposure. Three people died on the raft before the crew of the merchant ship *Celerina* rescued survivors six hours later. The most seriously injured were transferred to the Royal Canadian Navy aircraft carrier HMCS

*Bonaventure*. In all, forty-eight of the seventy-six people on board survived.

Art Gilbreth thinks he knows who his rescuer was. He experienced a sensation that he had a second "me." This superior existence was floating above him and could take in everything that was happening: the sinking plane, the raft, people in the water, and, finally, himself relative to all of that. "The me-above knew that the me-below existed, but the me-below did not know that the me-above existed. The me-above was giving instructions to me-below in the form of a low voice in my head." That voice, which told him to kick the silver thing, the tail fin, guided him to the safety of the raft.

Carmen Figueroa, however, was not sure about the source of her rescue. Afterward she searched through the entire passenger manifest and found no one named Toby or Tobias. They searched through the survivors and asked everyone rescued if they knew of a Toby. None did. Nor did anyone report seeing the young man she described. It was a mystery.

Was Toby an angel? Or did he emerge from her own automatic brain processes?

If it is the latter, then there is a contradiction here. The Angel Effect involves an unseen presence that gives people fresh and vital information that can help them and, in many instances, can directly aid their survival. Brian Shoemaker received very specific instructions, right down to the correct heading, which got him safely back to his base. Carmen Figueroa, lost in surging seas with no life raft in sight, also encountered a powerful friend in the form of a young man who called himself "Toby," a man who was not aboard that flight and whom nobody saw except her. He gave her encouragement and then told her what to do, commanding that she follow him. He led her straight to the lone raft.

If what happened to these people was an automatic brain response to extreme stress in a life-or-death situation, then this was the opposite of what happened to the Air France pilots. Instead of a survival strategy, they were feeling "out of control," at which point the brain freezes, and death ensues.

So which is it? Brain researchers advance two, seemingly irreconcilable neurological responses to situations of great stress and terror. One is brain freeze, which locks you into inaction. The other, the sensed presence, emerges from the unconscious brain, the product not of rational decisions but of base emotions and survival mechanisms. It takes command and, sometimes, your hand—literally—to lead you to safety.

But if the brain shuts down allowing for only instinctive behavior or "low-road emotions," then where is the fresh and intuitively correct information leading to survival really coming from? Does the brain somehow rally, creating a companion, providing the perfect way out of the situation? If that is the case, why didn't the pilots on Air France Flight 447 also experience what others do: the calm guidance of a benevolent presence? Why did one of them sit there, yanking on a stick, unable to contrive a way out of an impending disaster to which he was a leading contributor? Is it possible that for the pilots, the capacity to access the sensed presence had somehow been disabled? They were skilled commercial pilots. Perhaps training and experience had diminished their ability to discern help when it arrived, silencing those voices in them. Or if those voices were heard, they were not taken seriously.

To survive, they had to listen, and to listen they had to believe. Is that the explanation? Or were the highly specialized demands of their role as commercial pilots beyond the capability of "low-road" brain process to sort out? We will never know the answer. The black box that was recovered from the depths of the Atlantic Ocean and provided crucial evidence for French investigators told us what was going on inside the cockpit of Air France Flight 447, but it could not tell us what was going on inside those pilots' heads.

We do, however, know what was going on in Bill Haneke's head, because he survived against near-impossible odds to tell us, and this too illustrates how specific commands are given and how even the life of someone suffering near-fatal injuries can be saved.

WEST POINT GRADUATE Bill Haneke's crisis was certainly urgent. He was serving in Vietnam as an adviser in Binh Thuan Province, based in a compound centered around an old French hospital. The Viet Cong were active in the area, and Haneke and other American advisers, along with South Vietnamese troops, did their best to make their position safe. Even so, at one point the compound was overrun. Scores of people were killed, but Bill and a dozen others hid in a bunker and survived. Further attacks seemed inevitable. On November 13, 1968, Bill's commander ordered him to leave the compound to move two fifty-five-gallon fuel drums. His superior followed him, and the two went outside the gate briefly, with disastrous consequences. A Viet Cong soldier was lying in wait, and at a critical moment he detonated a mine that blasted a crater and propelled Haneke eighty feet through the air, leaving him dangling limply on a barbed-wire fence.

The twenty-six-year-old's injuries were grotesque. One eye was gone, and he had shrapnel in the other; his jaw was shattered, and bone and loose teeth obstructed his breathing. He suffered a head wound that exposed part of his brain. One leg had also been severed, as was part of the foot on his other leg. The carotid artery and jugular had been slashed, and with each heartbeat, blood would spurt out of his neck. He was aware that there had been an attack and that he was seriously hurt, but he couldn't see, could barely breathe and was clearly dying. He tried to move, but he felt paralyzed. It was as though he were beyond help. Believing that he was dying, Haneke prayed, "Oh, God, help me."[13]

Suddenly a soothing voice instructed him: "Turn your head to the left and relax. Have faith. I will help you through this."[14] He did as the voice said: he turned his head to the left, and this action partially staunched the flow of blood.

The explosion had alerted the entire compound, and several people ran to his aid, cutting him off the barbed wire. After about fifteen minutes a helicopter arrived with a medic. He received a tracheotomy to allow him to breathe more easily and was given plasma. What followed was a desperate forty-eight-hour fight for survival. Five times he was pronounced dead, and five times he defied seemingly impossible odds. At one point last rites were performed. Again he heard the voice urging him to remain calm. "I am with you," it said.

Bill was transferred to a series of field triages, finally arriving at an evacuation hospital in Long Binh. But the medical team could detect no breathing or pulse. He was beyond help. He was covered with a blanket, wheeled into a room, and left for dead. That might have been it, but once again he heard the same insistent voice, telling him that he would survive and that it would see him through it. "Give them a sign you are alive," the voice said. "It's very important you do this. Do it now!" it urged.

He tried to cry out but could make no discernible sound. Incredible pain washed over him. He summoned every little bit of strength left in him and jerked himself, causing an intravenous line to pull over the IV stand. "Hey, this guy's alive!" yelled a nurse. "Hey, doc, this guy's still kicking."[15] They rushed him into surgery. He spent fifteen hours on the operating table and two weeks in critical care before he was airlifted first to Japan and then to the Walter Reed Army Hospital in Bethesda, Maryland.

It took four years and some two hundred procedures, but eventually he recovered sufficiently to have some semblance of a normal life, eventually writing a book, *Trust Not*, about his military experiences and his astonishing story of survival. It is a deeply spiritual account of a profoundly spiritual experience. Asked what the source of the voice was, Bill says it came from God: "It was a divine voice, and although I thought I was dying, it did settle me down and I wasn't panicking quite as much."[16]

A REMARKABLY SIMILAR CASE, albeit of vastly different circumstances, occurred in a hospital in Lisburn in Northern Ireland. Donna Ferguson had just given birth to her fourth child, a daughter named Jessica. It was a normal pregnancy without complications, but afterward Donna felt extremely tired and dizzy. She had lost some blood but was not aware that she was suffering from a serious complication. Donna's husband, Gary, and a friend were visiting her when she felt in danger of passing out. They summoned a nurse, who decided she needed a good sleep; her doctor would see her during his morning rounds. Her visitors left, and Donna fell into a deep sleep.

Around 2 A.M. she began to hear a soft but insistent voice urging her to "wake up." She tried to ignore it, feeling she was too tired, but the voice persisted. "It never got angry, remaining calm as it repeatedly told me to wake up."[17] The voice did not stop there, however. "It told me to press the alarm." This would summon help to her bedside.

"I didn't even know there was an alarm. Still I couldn't open my eyes, but managed to find enough strength to lift my arm. Feeling a wire hanging next to me, I pressed the button. Fortunately, it was the alarm, which alerted the nurses."[18] One quickly arrived and discovered Donna had been hemorrhaging. "I was lying in a pool of blood and soon there were three nurses and a doctor crowded around my bed." They worked desperately to keep her awake, and Donna said she remembers telling a nurse that someone had woken her.

Donna was wheeled to a surgery and given a transfusion. She later discovered that a large part of the placenta had been left in the uterus. It was still contracting and pumping out blood to clear this away. The following day Donna told her physician that "someone had woken me, although I couldn't tell if it was a woman's or a man's voice, and he said it must have been my guardian angel, because if I'd lost much more blood, I wouldn't have survived."[19]

Are these simple cases of the low-road emotions overriding executive brain functions and essentially running amok?

People in these situations are no longer equipped to reason their way through desperate situations, so, the idea goes, the brain conjures up an alternative authority, the sensed presence, that helps them through it.

# - 7 -

# THE

# BALD

# WELDER

## EXTERNALIZED
## SECOND SELF

At age thirteen John Robbins was caught in extremely heavy surf that, he admits, he should have known better than to enter. He had been swimming all day at Big Corona Beach, on the south side of the entrance to Newport Harbor, California. It was late in the afternoon. The lifeguards had gone home. There were people farther down the beach, around fires, having picnics. But they were more than a hundred yards away. Robbins was still there because the surf had been good all day and he just couldn't pull himself away. His family beach house was visible at a distance of a quarter-mile on a bluff. All his friends had gone home already, and he was ready to do the same when he saw that a large set of waves was approaching the beach. The tempting challenge of the big surf was too much for John, who was lured back into the water.

From experience he knew the pattern of wave breaks is usually the same: they come in sets of three, with the third wave being the largest. A jetty, protecting the entrance to the adjacent harbor, protruded out into the ocean about a quarter-mile. The first incoming wave of this larger set of waves hitting the end of the jetty alerted him to their arrival, leaving him just enough time to scramble down to the water, dive in, swim out through the breaking white water of the first two waves, and be in position to catch the third and largest wave. "It was all standard practice for bodysurfing at this beach for experienced swimmers ... and I considered myself experienced, having bodysurfed for at least several years," he said.

When swimming out through surf, he would dive beneath the breaking white water rolling in toward the beach, thus avoiding being battered by the force of the incoming surge.

In this case, as the wall of white water drove toward him from the first wave, John realized that this was the largest surf he had ever encountered. He dove down as deep as he could, trying to get as flat as he could on the sandy seabed so as to avoid being thrown down against it by the force of the turbulent water above. Despite his efforts, however, the wave pummeled him.

"I was thrown about like a rag doll, smacking my head into the sand," he recalled. "It went on for much longer than I had ever experienced before. I was getting desperate for air." When he was finally able to surface, he gasped but instead took in a mouthful of water. "This caused me to cough and sputter, thus reducing my ability to get a good breath of air. I was in chest-high water, with an extremely strong riptide wanting to suck me further out to sea. I looked desperately at the shoreline, not more than forty yards away, for anybody to help me, but there was no one."

Robbins couldn't look for very long because the second and larger wave had broken, and its wall of white water, perhaps six to eight feet thick, was roaring toward him. "I had no choice, short of breath or not, to dive, or I would be terribly battered and broken by the force of the surf. Down I went, the thrashing even worse than with the first wave. I could not get back to the surface, my lungs were screaming for air, but I continued to be roiled about, unable to do anything but wait for the turbulence to subside. At last I was able to break the surface and gasp for air, but for the second time I gulped water instead of air, resulting in more choking and gasping."

At that moment, with the largest wave yet to hit, John feared he was about to die. "I was having flashes of my life, which seemed like an instant rerun of my entire life." Then, suddenly, a man appeared on a flimsy air mat, the sort of flotation device a child might use in a swimming pool. "You look like you could use some help—take ahold of this," the man said. John grabbed ahold, and almost immediately found himself gliding into the shore, on the leading edge of the white water of the third and largest wave. He said the sensation defied all logic. "Even if there was an air mat to hold on to, being hit by a wall of white water of that size would still thrash someone about with great ferocity." Instead, he glided breezily to shore, undisturbed by the wave crashing around him. He was deposited in shallow water, perfectly fine but exhausted. It took him a few moments to recover his breath. He sat at the water's edge, panting, his arms wrapped around his knees.

He then looked around for his rescuer. He wanted to thank the man who had saved his life but was astonished to discover there was no one there. In fact, "There was no one visible in either direction along the shoreline, nor was there anyone further back on the beach. There was no air mat. I was alone."

The mental vision of the man was so vivid that he felt he could pick him out of a lineup. He didn't look at all familiar to John: "He didn't look like he was an experienced beacher. His skin was white from little exposure to the sun. He seemed like a balding, middle-aged, somewhat paunchy working man, that maybe worked in a warehouse, or welding shop, a place that kept him out of the sun … but not an office worker, for some reason."

To this day John Robbins has no idea what happened to him at Big Corona Beach. He has thought about it many times. "I can generally accept the idea that experiences like this can generate an internal mechanism for survival that manifests as an external being. But how to explain the fact that I got to shore?"

His religious background is Protestant, although he had never really taken to it; church was more something that had to be endured. Still, the experience had all "the miraculous qualities of some of the Bible stories I had heard in Sunday school." His near-drowning and the miraculous rescue didn't make him any more religious, but it did leave him with an open mind. "There is no doubt in my mind that an external force intervened. Was it a guardian angel? I have no idea. He certainly didn't look the part."[1]

JIM PEACOCK WAS CAMPING in the Grebe Valley in New Zealand's Fiordland National Park. He was twenty-eight years old and had just finished grad school at Oregon State University. He had wanted to see New Zealand and decided that if he didn't take the trip then, his career would get busy and then he would likely never get another chance. It was his fifth day into the solo adventure and had been a perfect one, spent walking along the banks of the Grebe River, catching fish. He set up camp, then dove into his tent, tired but happy, and fell quickly to sleep.

At 3 A.M. Jim was awoken by water seeping into his tent. The night was pitch-black, so he reached for his flashlight and discovered that it was soaked and inoperable. He was able to find his waterproof matches and light a candle. The water was rising quickly, and some of his belongings began bobbing in his tent. He grabbed his clothes, stuffed his camera and lens into a plastic bag, and put everything he could salvage into his pack. There were still hours before daybreak, but he realized he had to get out of the tent and find some higher ground. By the time he crawled out, he was standing in boot-deep water. Rain was coming down in sheets.

Jim saw a tree nearby that was standing on slightly higher ground, so he grabbed his pack and made his way to it. He dropped his pack into a few inches of water and returned to dismantle the tent. He then used the tent fly to protect his pack and himself from the deluge. "Why? Why? Why is this happening?" he asked himself. It was bad enough that he had been caught in a flash flood deep in the wilderness, a fifteen-mile hike to the nearest community, but the darkness un-nerved him. The water was still rising. He was in the middle of a wide valley and knew he had to get to higher ground, but he could not see far enough to know which direction he should go. He opted to sit tight and wait for dawn. He had to tell himself: "Calm down Jim."

An hour passed, and there was still no light. The water level had risen noticeably. The air was chilly, and Jim huddled under his makeshift teepee, waiting. He lit his candle, and its faint light gave him some comfort. He kept repeating this pattern, crouching, telling himself to be patient, waiting for the light. A song entered his head, called "The Circle Game" by Joni Mitchell, and he drew comfort from it: "And the seasons they go 'round and 'round, and the painted ponies go up and down." Finally at 6 A.M., after three hours like this, he detected a faint light. It was enough. He blew out his candle, folded the tent, and looked at the scene that was unfolding as darkness lifted. "As far as I could see back to the hills on either side of the Grebe Valley was water," he said. "I had just walked down this beautiful fiord valley, fishing for rainbow trout." Now it was a lake.

Jim started walking, with the water up to his knees. He could not see where he was stepping, and he stumbled. A couple of more steps, and he found himself swimming with his backpack and fishing pole. He made his way back toward slightly higher ground, regaining his footing. But soon the water was up to his thighs, then his hips, then waist. Each step took him deeper and deeper into the surging water. It was not long before he was over his head and trying to keep afloat, grabbing hold of bushes. This process was repeated. He struggled out to higher ground, where the water was waist deep, then tried again to make for the valley walls, only to find himself swimming.

His sodden backpack was now a dead weight, and Jim realized that he had to abandon it. He tried to hang on to the fishing rod, which had been a gift, but he soon yielded that as well. Soaked to the bone and hypothermic, he realized he was now fighting not just to escape the water but for his life.

Jim swam for some bushes about twenty feet away, then tried to make his way through them, but the thorny vines seemed to grip him like predatory triffids. He had to stop and rip them from his legs. "Drowning … dying. … I'm not ready. Lord, I'm not ready. Please, please," Jim whispered. He reached a stretch of higher ground, where the water was only thigh deep. But it didn't last, and soon he was swimming again. He swam for a long time, perhaps an hour, over bushes and grabbing at trees, but there was still no ground. He wondered how long he could go on.

From time to time Jim would reach the branch of a large tree and pull himself out of the water to rest. The floodwaters surged around him, and he calculated the depth to be ten feet. He wanted just to stop and stay in a tree, but he feared the water would continue to rise; he had no idea how long he might be stranded. He couldn't imagine having to spend another night like this. "Can I stay here?" he asked himself. "No, I will die." He forced himself back into the water, and as he swam, "The Circle Game" again looped through his mind: "And the seasons they go 'round and 'round."

Finally he reached an open area that, the day before, had been a meadow. Until then he had been able to swim short distances before grabbing onto something to rest. This time, however, he would have to swim more than one hundred yards. He wasn't sure he could do it but felt he had no choice. About halfway across the open water, exhausted, he rolled onto his back, thinking he'd float for a minute to try to catch his breath. But when he tried, he realized his boots and his wool clothing weighed him down, temporarily pulling him under.

Jim struggled to the surface and resumed his swim, but after a short distance his foot caught on something, probably a vine. He again went under the water. He got water in his mouth and could not free his legs. "I felt like someone grabbed my legs and was pulling me down, under the surface." He swallowed more water. His struggle seemed hopeless. He admitted to himself he would have to give up. Then, "A wonderful warm feeling went through my entire body," he said. He was warm for the first time in hours. His life began to pass before his eyes, in rapid succession—family, friends, his cottage, his mother very distinctly. "God, what will she think," he thought. He felt he was dead.

And then not. He doesn't know what happened. Perhaps by giving up the fight, the vines released him. Throughout all of this, Jim was talking to God, "asking for help." He had been raised a Roman Catholic, but he was not practicing and was not a deeply religious person. He had spiritual beliefs, but they were more tied to nature than any particular religion. Maybe God answered his prayers, he thought, as he suddenly bobbed to the surface, spitting out water.

Then, as he gasped for air, "I actually 'saw' Jesus in a boat, floating by me." The figure was standing in a boat and exuded a sense of peace. It was a vivid sensation that Christ was there, so real that he actually felt he could see Him, but then not in the conventional way. He did have an image of Him nonetheless. "All I know is I had a conversation with Him and asked Him for strength."[2] The presence responded, and he knew he would have the strength he needed to survive. He realized, "I'm getting out."[3]

Jim has no doubt why he survived. "I am convinced that this 'third man' or Jesus or a spirit saved my life. I believe now this person helped me from drowning. At that time he gave me a feeling of comfort and confidence," he said, a belief that he could overcome the danger and survive.

Now dog-paddling, he continued across the open water. His arms felt like lead. He didn't think he could swim farther. But something allowed him to continue, and at last he reached a bush and grabbed ahold of it. After resting briefly, clinging on, he swam farther, reaching the branch of a tree. Again, he debated staying in the tree, but again he thought he would not last long. Instead, he reasoned that the major work was behind him, and the swim now involved short distances, from tree to bush or tree, so he continued. At one point he grabbed hold of a floating tree, which acted as a life preserver. With time his feet touched bottom, and after slogging along the water on foot for a time, he at last dragged himself out and onto land.

At first he was unable to walk. Twice he tried to stand up, but he couldn't. He was hypothermic and wanted to sleep by the lake, but he forced himself to fight his way up the steep fiord, at least six hundred feet, up to a service road that would lead to Monowai Village, the nearest community. He found that an idea had been placed in his head, a thought that he kept falling back on for support: "Don't deal with anything until it is right in front of you." He felt that the figure in the boat had placed this thought in his head. Finally, he reached the top and saw the road, but it had been washed out and was impassible—there would be no vehicles coming along to collect him.

At noon he sat down beside a power pole. He wanted desperately to sleep and started to drift, but he was afraid to let go of consciousness. He was hypothermic, still soaked, and knew he had to keep moving. Finally, after struggling along the road, through mudslides sometimes waist-deep, he finally saw a roof in the distance and could see a car parked outside. He walked up to the cabin and knocked. A woman saw him and cried out, "Come in!" Her husband soon arrived. All Jim could say was "I need help!" It was 1 P.M. It had taken him seven hours to reach help. He later learned that the rainstorm that hit Grebe Valley that night and day was a greater than one hundred–year event. It was a miracle—quite literally as far as he was concerned—that Jim Peacock had survived.

At the most difficult moment of his struggle, when he had given up and nearly drowned, when he saw his life pass before his eyes and asked for God's help, that man in a boat had given him what he needed to live. "I have always felt like it was Jesus, but never really have been able to explain what I saw. Few days go by when I don't think about the day when I nearly died and I saw a man in a boat who guided me to safety and saved my life."

PAT FRASCOGNA IS A successful lawyer and community leader in his home town. In 1990 Frascogna was founder and president of the state Tournament of Roses Association and helped raise $100,000 in private donations to build a state float for the parade in Pasadena.[4] As president of his state's Sports Council, Frascogna helped bring several NFL exhibition games to his state. In 1997 he ran unsuccessfully for mayor of his town. His major focus, however, was on building a successful law practice and a family.

Frascogna, his wife, and their children enjoyed an affluent lifestyle. His material expectations grew with his income. They lived in a nice home, owned a second property, and drove nice cars, including a Corvette. But in 2007 Frascogna noticed a "tightening" around his law practice. There was less work, and as the financial crisis deepened, the financial stress became severe. By early 2009, like many other Americans, he was confronted with the possibility of foreclosure on his house. A car was repossessed. The IRS came after him. The situation was, he said, "just horrible," and the strain on his family was palpable.

The financial difficulties gave rise to marital difficulties. As Frascogna put it: "Eventually just about everything in our lives seemed to be difficult and uncertain." Then, in the midst of this situation, he intervened in a dispute that ended up with Frascogna accidentally breaking his nose, an injury that required surgery. Late in May 2010 he got into the Jacuzzi tub in the middle of the night and began to cry and didn't stop for two hours. A sense of frustration and hopelessness overcame him. The entire situation seemed overwhelming. He felt like he was losing the life that he had worked so hard to build, and there was nothing he could do about it.

Two weeks later, in the first week of June, he was working at his home computer one weekday. He was doing nothing out of the ordinary, and no one else was home. He suddenly felt a presence, behind him, and when he looked he saw his father, Frank. Frascogna says what he saw is very difficult to explain, but that the image was "more like when a person sees someone in their peripheral vision. In other words you see them and, thus, know they are there, but because you are not looking at them directly the visual aspect of their presence is not the focus."[5]

His father had died in 1987 at age sixty-five. Frank Frascogna served in World War II and had been at Utah Beach. He ended the war with the rank of major and became a petroleum geologist. He was a man of average build but "was a giant to all who knew him," said Pat. "He was the embodiment of the American spirit." Pat Frascogna had always measured himself against his father "and firmly believe that if I ever become even half the man he was then I will have done well." Now his father was standing not more than eight feet away, and Pat was a man faced with defeat.

His father's return did not scare Pat; it puzzled him: "I looked at him for five or so seconds before getting up and walking away from him to a window in the room. I then turned around and saw him still standing there just as he was before. Frank never spoke to me, nor me to him." But Pat knew exactly why his father was there with him. The experience lent him comfort, and not only during the ninety or so seconds that his father's presence was with him in the study. "He had always been stalwart in my eyes, and at the time he appeared, it was to impart that to me." As he put it: "I know he was there to represent strength."

Frascogna said it was not the same as having a person standing in the room with him. "The best way I can describe it is that I believe he was there; when I sensed a presence that day it was indeed him. I believe that in some fashion my mind produced a familiar image of him for me to 'see.' Nevertheless, there is no question he was indeed there."

In time Pat was able to rebuild his law practice. The financial pressure eased; the crisis, for Pat Frascogna, had ended. The turning point came when the presence appeared and gave him strength to continue.

ANOTHER CURRENT SCIENTIFIC THEORY is that the sensed presence is an extracorporeal extension of our sense of self, and this has become the "dominant neuropsychological view."[6] Somehow distortions of the conscious self create the sensation of another you, which conflicts with the brain's single-body image. We all have a brain-generated portrait of ourselves—our arms and hands, our torso, back, and head. This "knowledge" of our body, functioning for the most part unconsciously, guides us as we move about physical space and interact with other people. It is how we know where we end and another person begins. Knowing that there can be only one you, "If for any reason your brain is tricked (or altered or damaged) into thinking that there is another you—an internal doppelganger—this inevitably conflicts with your single-body schema," explains Michael Shermer, adding that the brain then explains this anomaly by assigning the status of a fully externalized being to this sensation of another you. Because it can't be you, it has to be someone else.

In the case of John Robbins, that meant that during the process of drowning, panic and stress evoked a reduplication of himself that offered to help him (we are, for the most part, concerned for our own well-being). According to this theory, in essence, John helped himself, but his brain attributed the help to another person, even a very unlikely other—a pale, paunchy man bobbing on a flimsy air mattress. It was not actual help, then, but instead the idea of external help, incited by a life-or-death struggle, that aided John's ability to help himself.

This idea can be applied to so many of the people in this book. Pat Frascogna, then, could have been comforting himself in a moment of personal crisis. All that was happening to these people was a change in how their body was represented in their brain, with the result that an externalized self was created that tricked them into believing that an external agency was helping them; instead, they were simply drawing on their own inner resources. They were, in effect, their own guardian angels, deriving power and receiving wisdom from within. They were helping themselves.

There is evidence to support this hypothesis. In some cases people will report that the presence seems to imitate their own movements. Often the presence is very familiar, and its intentions are instantly recognized as benevolent. In rare cases, like that of Art Gilbreth, the survivor of the North Atlantic ditching, the rescuer is even recognized as a second and superior "me."

AN ACCIDENTAL DISCOVERY at a Swiss hospital lends credence to the theory. In order to treat a young woman for epilepsy, neurosurgeons implanted a number of electrodes, then stimulated her brain to try to localize where her seizures originated. When the stimulus was applied to her temporoparietal junction, she turned her head to the side. The stimulus was removed, and when it was resumed she turned her head again. When she was asked why she was turning her head, she replied that she had experienced a "strange sensation" of something nearby. Then, when it was reapplied, she said, "It's not really something; it's a person I feel."[7] She said that this somebody was right behind her. According to one of the researchers, Olaf Blanke, the woman "used the word shadow to actually refer to it, which is a strange choice because a shadow is something you see." To test this relationship between the twenty-two-year-old woman's body position and the "illusory shadow person," further tests were conducted, and the sensation always seemed to match her own position.

Blanke noted that electrodes were implanted in the patient in the parietal and the temporal cortex as well as the junction between them. "When we stimulated we could induce the feeling of a presence almost as if turning on and off a light switch," the researchers reported. The temporoparietal junction organizes sensory information and our sense of self. As Blanke explains it: "The parietal lobe is encoding my body in space, my arm position, my trunk position, my head position; it is a region specialized for this, and this is automatic, unconscious. The temporal lobe is a structure specialized for the environment, this room, and the social world around me, and to embed my body position with the rest of the environment."

By stimulating this brain structure, then, the young woman felt a presence so vivid that she was able to identify it as young and, eventually, to confirm its sex as male. Yet it was lacking that which invests these experiences with their power and meaning, the key aspect of these experiences: intentionality. At one point she said the feeling was unpleasant, but it didn't evoke strong emotion either way, negative or positive. It was not a benevolent being; it was a nullity. This is the critical difference between her case and those that occur spontaneously, outside the clinical setting.

John Robbins not only felt the presence of another person, but that person even communicated with him. He knew the man was there to help him. The body-image hypothesis fails to explain these kindly intentions fully. If we accept that this could have been John failing to recognize his own externalized self's desire to help himself, how do we explain the fact that he had an image of what that person looked like?

And if it was a visual hallucination, why would it not resemble himself? It is possible that in recalling the event later, he embellished it with descriptive details. If this is the case, the presence, therefore, became a paunchy welder or warehouse worker. But then there's that other problem: How did this other self succeed in transporting him safely to shore? After all, John was defeated. He felt he was going to die. The largest of the three waves was breaking and about to take him. How is it that despite this he was able to glide safely to shore? It takes a lot to credit a distortion of his sense of self, which caused him to reach deep inside to call upon inner reserves to help himself, with such a rescue.

There is an enduring mystery surrounding all of these reports. A simple disruption in the processing of body-self information might have created the sense of an externalized being, just as it might have provided subtle cues as to the age and sex of the presence. But how can it have created a powerfully benevolent being or one imbued with the capacity to save a life?

KEVIN GILLEN WAS WORKING as a firefighter in New Rochelle, New York, when, on the afternoon of May 16, 2006, he responded to an automatic alarm in the city's downtown. These alarms are usually false, but on this occasion Gillen arrived at the scene to discover flames shooting across Main Street from a storefront. It was a five-story multi-use building, with retail on the ground floor and apartments above. People were fleeing the building by using a fire escape, and smoke was billowing out of every opening in the structure.

Gillen was on the engine crew that day. They pulled a large diameter hose off the fire engine and got water on the seat of the fire until they reached the point where the building could be entered and an attempt made to rescue people who might be trapped inside. The fire was still burning, but the intensity was subdued, and the chief told Gillen to grab a partner and search the upper floors for anyone who might be trapped or who might have succumbed to the smoke.

Firefighters work in pairs, and so after he reached the stairway he waited for his partner to arrive with a thermal imaging camera. Kevin was anxious, however, and after a few moments he started up a couple of steps, getting a head start, when he heard someone screaming out for help through violent fits of coughing. Gillen's partner was not yet there, but he decided to go and get the person, thinking both that time was critical and that it would be an easy rescue ... go up and come straight back down. "What could go wrong?" he asked himself.[8]

Continuing up the stairs, Gillen reached the floor where the voice was coming from. He dropped to his knees and crawled down the hallway, avoiding the thickest smoke. He passed through a couple of doorways, following the desperate pleas for help. There was limited visibility, and the air was filled with super-heated gases as well as carbon monoxide, which replaces oxygen. Without a breathing apparatus, you cannot breathe for long in such conditions. When he reached the victim, the man shouted, "I am gonna die!" He was clearly in desperate shape. He was frantic because he couldn't breathe. Gillen had a split second to react.

"I thought I would be able to just turn around and get out, so I did the unthinkable: I took off my mask and put it on the victim." It was an act of compassion and of heroism, but it was risky, and it is not what firemen are trained to do in such situations; they are not supposed to remove their own masks. "I turned and pulled him with me to what I thought was the hallway." But he soon realized it was a dead end. He had become disoriented. He later found out he had entered a walk-in closet.

Gillen now found that he himself could not breathe. "My life sort of flashed past, and I realized this is it. This is how I die." He fought back, trying to think about how to get out. "And as I started to think about what to do, I heard someone say 'Kevin!' and I just sort of moved around a wall where I thought the voice came from." He immediately recognized what the source of the voice was and that "it was coming from where I needed to go," but more than that, he actually felt a physical presence; he felt it was the presence of God.[9]

Despite what was happening around him, his name was spoken with perfect clarity. He followed the voice, he knew it represented help, and yet he thought he was going deeper into the apartment. But he didn't doubt it, and in fact it led him back to the hallway. A short time later "I saw my partner coming and I figured he must have yelled for me." Gillen escaped, barely, and the man he rescued survived.

Kevin was hospitalized for a day, and it wasn't until later that he thought about the voice again, and the more he did, the stranger it seemed to him. His partner, Dan, was not even at the middle point of a long staircase, and besides, he was wearing a mask. Even when standing right next to a person wearing such a mask, hearing them and making out what they're saying is difficult. In addition, Dan never called Kevin by his given name, and the voice had. "I am called 'LU' which is short for Lieutenant, or 'Gillen,' which is my last name. No one on our job calls me Kevin." So he decided to ask Dan whether he had called out for him that day. The answer was no.

This only confirmed what he already suspected. Said Kevin: "I realized that I must have heard the voice of God drawing me out."

IN THE EARLY EVENING of October 1, 2011, Brian Lumley and his friend Paul were traveling in an inflatable dinghy powered by an outboard motor across Toronto's harbor. They were making the short 1.9-nautical-mile jaunt to visit a friend on Algonquin Island, one in the small group of Toronto islands. The skies were overcast, winds were easterly, and there was a light chop in the lake for the twenty-five-minute journey. The two men visited their friend Sue at her cabin on the island. Her father, Neil, was also there, and they all had a couple of glasses of wine over the course of three hours before Brian and Paul carried on to the Queen City Yacht Club, which was having its awards night. Brian had a drink and was soon dancing with a woman he'd just met. Paul also had a drink. They stayed there for a little over an hour, until midnight, when the band stopped playing and the party started to wind down. They decided to head back.

The night was pitch-black and overcast but, Brian says, "not too windy or stormy. Both of us had made the trip at night and in foul weather several times. We thought nothing of it." Paul was driving from the port stern position, and Brian was sitting forward on the starboard side to balance the dinghy. As they headed out, fog started to roll in, but they continued on, around the Ward's Island ferry entrance light. Brian reminded Paul that there was a boat anchored in the bay, and Paul acknowledged that and adjusted his course slightly. Visibility was quickly worsening, however, and the fog was now thick and lights from the shore were not visible. Brian mentioned the fog to Paul as they shot out into what he described as "black on black."

"We knew the main hazard we were dealing with was the Eastern Gap breakwater wall, which was at least a couple hundred yards long and ran north into the harbor off the east end of Ward's Island," says Brian. The wall is unlit on the west side, the side they were approaching. He has no memory of what happened next, although, judging by his injuries, he believes they struck the breakwater wall with the starboard side of the dinghy, and he was "thrown forward hitting the wall with my right side and was probably bounced back into the water." He believes this is what happened because he had wounds on the right side of his head and down the right side of his body.

He was knocked unconscious and is unsure for how long. He was floating in the water in his Salus Antigua floater coat, a foul-weather coat the design of which has a floatation device built in, as the name suggests. Brian came to, and "I believe I was talking when I came to in the water, but I don't know how much." He also didn't know who he was talking to. He passed out again, then "I remember regaining consciousness looking straight up into the sky; it was still deep night with fog, so it was a murky void to me—no stars, no moon. I was disoriented, in a lot of pain, I could not see properly, I was soaking wet, I was floating, and I had no idea why," he recalled. After that, he drifted back into unconsciousness.

Sometime later he came to and felt very cold and in extreme pain but a little more aware—aware, for example, that he had to get out of the water, but then he slipped away again. This process repeated itself, but each time he was a little more alert. He moved his head and noticed the hood on his floater coat had kept his face above water. He turned his head each way, but doing so caused the pain to intensify. He did, however, make out the shape of a long pier. He recovered sufficiently to realize he had to save himself.

Brian wondered why he had been left in the water and where Paul was. He started working his way toward the long shadow, finally reaching the breakwater wall. He reached up, trying to grab the top with his right arm. He got enough of a hold to reach up with his left arm; eventually he found niches, cracks, and breaks in the concrete, and like a climber he held on and began the struggle to climb out of the water. Given the severity of his injuries, it was a near-impossible task. It was then that he felt as if he were pushed. He had literally been helped out of the water. "As far as I'm concerned Paul shoved me." He looked back but could not see Paul or the dinghy.

Brian crawled a short distance. He was shaking violently, and he threw up. He started to faint but caught himself and found a tuft of soft grass and placed his head gently on it. Someone told him he needed to move, he was concussed, and "I was afraid of going into shock." So he began to crawl again, and eventually he pulled himself up to his feet. He says a presence of someone, he called it "the pilot," guided him to a path and led him down it. It was still night, and he could not see any lights. He did soon see the outlines of some cottages, and he called out for help several times, but no one answered and the cottages remained dark. The pilot guided Brian toward Sue's boat, which was now close. "A being encouraged me along and got me to think about my life and immediate plans, how I needed shelter fast before my system began to fail."

With the pilot's help, he located the boat easily and broke the companionway lock with the boat's transmission shifting bar. "I was talking to someone and taking advice." It was still before dawn. He removed his soaked outwear and climbed into her bedding. He still remembers speaking to the pilot, but at some point his helper went silent and Brian passed out, remaining there until 9:30 A.M., when he awoke briefly and checked his watch. He thought he heard voices outside the boat and tried to stand up, but he fell over. "My head was in great pain, and I was still feeling hypothermic." The voices had disappeared before he could collect himself, and he slumped back into sleep for several more hours.

When he awoke again he immediately headed toward Sue's house, which was not very far away. "All this time I was trying to figure out where Paul was, and I was going over possible scenarios, none of which made any sense. I would not entertain the possibility he was dead." When Brian reached Sue's house a home-care worker looking after Sue's father, Neil, who was seriously ill, told him Sue had left for the mainland. She wouldn't let Brian into the house. Eventually she agreed to try to call Sue on her cell phone. Neil was summoned, but even though he was chatting with Brian the night before, he failed to recognize him: "He didn't recognize me because of the condition I was in, and he couldn't understand a word I was saying."

Police were summoned, and he was questioned for a while before an ambulance arrived and took him to Mount Sinai Hospital, where he was treated and released. Paul was not nearly so lucky. Brian believes that on impact the dinghy likely flexed, so "Paul was thrown from the port side through the air hitting the wall with the added force of the slingshot effect. I believe they found Paul in the water near the shore. Paul suffered a severe skull fracture. It sounded to me like he had drowned quickly, within moments of the impact."

Brian does not know how he was pushed out of the water or who or what had led him to safety. "It is possible I was just helping myself, I guess. But it didn't seem that way. It seemed to me like I had outside help. That's why I'm alive."

IN THE LATE MORNING of October 11, 2007, a light plane carrying three people crashed into a hillside in Portage Pass, Alaska. The pass had been socked in with clouds, and a powerful wind shear had hit the single-engine Piper. When the engine then stalled, the aircraft spiraled down, crashing at an angle, nose in. The impact pushed the engine into the pilot's lap, killing him. One of the passengers also died instantly. The only other person in the aircraft, Ann Witherspoon, was thrown forward and hit the dash. But, although her face was bloodied, she remained conscious. The plane then erupted into flames, and Ann fought to escape, but her left leg was caught in her seatbelt. When she untangled it she fell backward out of the plane and watched it burn.

Ann suffered burns on her face and hands as well as cuts to her face. One of her eyes was full of blood. She had lost several teeth. She had miraculously survived a plane crash, yet her chances still seemed bleak. Ann was stranded at the foot of Portage Glacier, fifty miles from Anchorage. No flight plan had been filed, she knew, there was no transponder, and they had flown against the advice of the weather duty officer at Anchorage airport: "I knew no one would be looking for us." She began to climb up a rugged cliff, by now feeling very weak. Finally reaching the top, she sat down to rest. Periodically, a plane would fly over, and she would wave frantically, screaming at the top of her lungs, but these planes were flying too high up for anyone to have a realistic chance of seeing her.

She then abruptly felt as though an "external force was putting thoughts into my head." It was a presence, and it advised her to go back to the site of the wrecked aircraft. It wasn't an audible voice, but it was emphatic.

Ann immediately got up and followed the instruction. It took her about an hour and a half to climb back down to the crash site. She felt like a robot—just following this persistent thought. Although she could not see the wreckage, she knew the presence was guiding her. When she worried that she would become dehydrated, the presence encouraged her to stop to drink meltwater flowing off the Portage Glacier. The icy water also helped numb the pain of the injuries she had sustained in the crash.

Assuming that she would die of exposure that night, Ann became obsessed with the idea that she should at least prevent wild animals from eating her remains. So when she finally made it back to the wreck, she built a shelter under the one undamaged wing of the aircraft. Through it all, the presence stayed with her. She conversed with it at times, but at other times she just had a strong feeling that a friend was there. She derived great comfort from its company and gained a measure of peace, despite retaining the belief that she was going to die.

She found a bag of clothing belonging to the pilot and changed clothes; hers had been singed and were wet from blood and ice water. She created a "nest" under the wing and felt she had done everything she could have done to survive, when she heard a dog barking. The presence then left.

Suddenly a little boy emerged from the trees, accompanied a moment later by his uncle. The man introduced himself as Dwayne, appeared startled, and asked, "What are you doing here?" Ann replied, "We crashed." He studied the wreckage briefly, and, seeing the charred corpse of the pilot, sent the boy ahead for help. He then took Ann's arm and helped her walk down the pass. She asked why they were out hiking on such a cold and miserable day. Dwayne said the boy had insisted. Ann became convinced that the presence had instigated their strange, uncharacteristic hike, that they had been summoned to her side. Soon rescue workers arrived, and she was taken to hospital.

The presence that urged her down the mountainside, back to the crash scene was critical to Ann's rescue: "The FAA later told me that they couldn't figure out why I was alive, that the crash was 'unsurvivable.' I felt the presence all that day and felt that I was being directed by it. I talked to it frequently. I believe that the presence actually sent that little boy out there to find me. That he too was directed by it."[10] Like all the rest, she believed it to be someone else, an existence separate from her own. She does not accept that she was her own rescuer.

# ROSA PARKS'S TWIN

## GUARDIAN ANGEL

AT AGE SIX, PHIL TAYLOR AND HIS TWO BROTHERS BE-
came the first African American students at a Catholic
school in Cincinnati. The year was 1959, and the family had
just moved into the area. Their experience with integration
was nothing short of disastrous. Phil didn't know what
racism was until he started at that school. There, other kids
taunted him and beat him up. "Recess quickly became an exercise—an exercise in watching your back. Kids screaming in
your face names and words that you did not understand."[1] In
their own way, some of the teachers were as bad as the students. One of Phil's brothers told him that he "would no
longer raise his hand in his class because the teacher would
never call on him." His other brother was made to clean up
another child's mess. Phil didn't feel there was anyone at the
school he could turn to.

The boy put up with the daily ordeal and continued to attend classes for a time, but then he started to slip away and
return home early. His mother would ask him: "What's
wrong? Why are you running away from school?" But Phil
didn't have the words to describe what he was going through,
so he just cried. One day he left the school and ran for his
home. He thought he knew the route, but after a while he
found himself alongside a six-lane expressway. He realized he
had made a wrong turn, so he stopped at the side of the busy
road. "I stood there in frigid weather, nose wet, watching the
cars and trucks whiz by at 60 or 70 miles per hour."

Rather than retrace his steps, Phil thought if there was a
break in the traffic and if he ran fast enough, he would be
able to safely reach the other side and somehow pick up the
trail home. It was a dangerous calculation, but he was too

young to know that. "The truth is that my small body would have been smashed and tossed by vehicle after vehicle," Phil recalled. Just then, as the boy's muscles tensed, and he readied to make the dash, "an elderly woman's hand locked onto my shoulder. I remember vaguely that she was black and small and wore the same kind of clothes my grandmother wore."

The woman asked Phil what he was doing, and he explained that he was going to cross the six lanes of heavy traffic. He never made the attempt. "She said I would have been killed." What is more, it was as if she was aware of the torment he was experiencing at school. She buttoned his jacket up, pulled his hat over his ears, and took his hand. He did not know who the woman was, but years later recognized her as a "dead-ringer for Rosa Parks," the brave woman who refused to give up her bus seat to a white passenger and thus provoked the Montgomery, Alabama, bus boycott that in turn helped spark the civil rights movement in the United States. Phil Taylor said he could engage in lengthy "theological discussions regarding the events of that day" but really has no interest in doing so because it would not change the facts. "The woman consoled me, as if she knew what was really going on inside me. I told her everything ... but she seemed to already know. She took me home and then ... disappeared. She had intervened and saved my life. She was my guardian angel."[2]

**BRITISH NEUROLOGIST** Macdonald Critchley wrote a groundbreaking study titled, "The Idea of a Presence" in 1955. Critchley is one of few scientists to have made even passing reference to the guardian angel in relation to the phenomenon or, indeed, to acknowledge that it might have any spiritual significance whatsoever. He said the fact that people who encounter a sensed presence will often consider it a guardian angel is "not surprising. ... The 'Guardian Angel' motif is inescapable to those with strong beliefs."[3] He alluded to the long tradition of such interventions, reaching back to the Bible and Psalm 91: "He will give his angels charge of you / to guard you in all your ways. / On their hands they will bear you up, / lest you dash your foot against a stone."

But the concept is still more ancient than that, having been traced at least as far back as Zoroastrianism. Their angelology was absorbed into Jewish practice in Babylonia and subsequently inherited by Christianity and Islam, both of which have their own traditions of guardian angels. As Critchley wrote, "The notion of an *angelo custode* is a common teaching and is depicted in religious art as an angel with a wide wingspan standing as an unseen protector behind a little child." An unseen protector standing behind a little child—but also standing behind us all.

Thomas Aquinas, in his *Summa Theologiae* (written 1265–1274), helped to fill in some of the gaps in our knowledge of angels. To begin, it is not true that anything goes; there are certain rules that govern the appearance of guardian angels. He wrote that angels are incorporeal and that they are spirit, not matter, so they are invisible. Yet they can assume bodies and thereby become visible, and, though immaterial, they have the power to move matter. Their presence can be felt or not, and their voice heard or not. In other words, they can be quite hard to pin down.

What is more, the powers of angels, though great, are also prescribed, Aquinas says. They cannot alter the will of human beings. Thus, they basically have to work with what they've been given. Of course, they can influence us by presenting various enticements and rewards that lead us down the path of virtuousness. They can also affect our imagination and temperament and can work upon the human senses, guiding and "instigating." But they cannot lead us by the nose or force us to make the right decision. To a certain degree, their hands are tied.[4]

Aquinas teaches that each human being has his or her own guardian angel from birth, not baptism, so no one faith is singled out for this care. Their primary role is to illuminate, not to protect. "Sometimes, however," he noted, "beyond the general law, they appear visibly to human beings, by an exceptional favor (or grace) of God, similarly to how miracles happen beyond the order of nature."

Aquinas established a theory of angels, with its own mechanics and hierarchy. However, one recent study, "Angelic Belief as American Folk Religion," takes a contrary view, arguing, "angelic spirits are typically informal, unsystematic, and anecdotal." Even so, that study argued, angels serve a useful function insofar as they "provide compelling narratives and potential explanations for complex real-world events … they are a conduit for interaction between material and immaterial in the minds of believers, typically serving their needs without demanding anything in return. As such, they are cognitively and emotionally appealing figures."[5]

Not all see it that way, however. Given their intangible nature, skeptics tend to see angel reports as a sort of catchall explanation for oddball or otherwise mysterious experiences.

According to the "angel" entry in the *Skeptics Dictionary*: "Literally anything *could* be an angel and any experience *could* be an angel-experience. The existence of angels cannot be disproved. The down side of this tidy picture is that angels cannot be proved to exist, either. Everything that *could* be an angel could be something else. ... Belief in angels, angel sightings and angel experiences is entirely a matter of faith."[6]

One study of guardian angels takes it further, detecting a pattern that exists in angelic rescues and uses the example of miraculous car rescues to illustrate the point. At the moment of crisis, the study noted, the angel makes itself known. "It appears as a 'hunch,' a soft but clear inner voice directing the driver, as a commanding outer voice ... as a superhuman figure that only the car's occupant can see ... [or] the mysterious figure—police officer with unregistered badge, tow truck driver, 'unassuming Hispanic man'—who appears to wake, warn, or guide."[7] Here it is argued that following a near-death experience, the driver tries to reconstruct events and "realizes that the sensation or apparition must have been an angel, that the special condition of emergency revealed a direct communion with angelic order." They then produce as evidence what the paper terms "negative proof" in the form of the disappearance of the angelic rescuer. As positive proof, they will also describe a sense of "peace" or "reassurance" and sometimes "the feeling of no longer being alone."

Many of the cases in this book might fit this model. But take as an example Erich Brinkmeyer's experience. He was driving in the middle of the night on Missouri Highway 50 near Drake, Missouri, when he passed out behind the wheel. His car cartwheeled off the road and landed in a cornfield. When he finally came to, seriously injured, a woman, blonde, in her twenties, and wearing white clothes, came to his aid. She stayed with him, comforted him, tended to his injuries, and urged him to stay awake in the event of a concussion. When she did leave, she said it was to summon help and ensure he reached safety. When the Missouri State Highway Patrol later reached Erich, he inquired as to the identity of his rescuer, whose comfort and advice was so critical to his survival. But police had no record of anyone reporting an accident. It was, he is convinced, "an angelic encounter."

Janet Venendez's experience in 1997 was also similar to the model. Janet was about to board the subway in downtown New York City. The platform was curved. The aged IRT Battery Place subway train had no straps to hold on to and its floor was greasy. Entering the car, Janet slipped, and her left leg became wedged between the train and the platform. The twenty-seven-year-old screamed, but if anyone heard, they did not respond. The train conductor's bell rang twice. She struggled but only slipped farther, up to her thigh. The doors then shut. Her leg was still wedged in the gap, with her other leg splayed on the platform. Janet's heart was pounding, and she prayed that her death would be instantaneous. With her leg severed, she assumed she would immediately lose consciousness and die. Then, suddenly, she felt the presence of a man, and she somehow knew he possessed superhuman strength. It all happened in a moment: she felt as though she was lifted up like a child, the door opened, and she was laid inside the car. Except that the man who had aided her was nowhere to be seen. None of the people around her were responsive or interested in her plight, nor did any of them appear to have seen her rescuer. Janet says she was the recipient of a "spiritual gift," and that was enough. She feels now that "my angel walks with me every day."

The critique argues that descriptions of angels in miraculous rescues are often "vague and stunningly vacuous." What is emphasized is not the character of the angel but rather the concept: "The writers seem almost wary of being too specific; the very presence of the feeling, like the very presence of the angel, is what they want to emphasize." The facts of what happened leading up to the encounter are set out in exacting, almost excruciating, detail, and each moment is analyzed frame by frame, as if a slow-motion film. However, the most important aspect of the experience, the angel itself, remains insubstantial, frustratingly so. This means that even people who are convinced that they encountered angels close up are unable to shed much light on them. The angels remain a blank canvas.

There is another even greater problem with angelic rescues. As the playwright Tony Kushner, author of the play *Angels in America,* told *Time* magazine: "The question is, why are you saved with your guardian angel and not the woman who was shot to death shielding her children in Brooklyn three weeks ago?"[8] That is a difficult question, but in fact Aquinas provided an answer to this, albeit a not entirely satisfactory one. He taught that "Sometimes, in the workings of providence, a man must suffer trouble; this is not prevented by the guardian angel." Mike Aquilina in his book *Angels of God,* sets it out succinctly: "Our guardian angel's task is to get us to heaven—not to keep us or our loved ones from suffering or death. After all, suffering is perhaps the principle means of our spiritual growth on earth, and death is our final portal to God. ... We should not be surprised when friends, or even children, die in accidents. Nor should we see it as some sort of angelic malfunction."[9]

This is a hard concept to get one's head around. Even if one accepts the premise that horrible accidents, the deaths of young people, of infants like James, of good people, you name it—all the carnage that is wrought on human beings— are spiritual growth opportunities, it is still difficult to believe that our guardian angels, though capable of intervening to save lives, may not do so because the angel sees the bigger picture and has an overarching responsibility to deliver us for judgment. Apparently this imperative trumps even the need to keep us physically in one piece. Depending upon the circumstances, this could be seen as fickle to even the most devout person and could well serve as a test of faith.

But as Mike Aquilina said, "The angels ... know God's mind better than we do. They know when an injury or illness will draw us closer to God." And there are plenty of instances when they do intervene, because it is not someone's time or someone still has something to accomplish on earth. "We should have no doubt that angels do intervene for us, sometimes very directly," Aquilina commented.

There are plenty of people who are prepared to attest to that.

NORA LAM WAS A YOUNG CHILD during the Japanese occupation of Shanghai during the Second World War, but she was not too young to register the brutality of that occupation. Every afternoon on her way home from her Christian missionary–run school she was witness to atrocities, and in her memoir, *China Cry*, she described what she saw: "I would run all the way home from school, past the rotting bodies hanging from the trees, past Japanese soldiers whipping old rickshaw men into the dust—bayoneting them if they cried out."[10] She saw lines of starving people waiting for their meager rations. All of this was a lot for a child to take in.

But the cruelty of her older cousins when she reached her grandmother's home was what crystallized her sense of isolation and fear. They would lock Nora outside, telling her to go to the back door, then, once there, sending her back to the front. They would do this repeatedly, despite the real danger any child faced outside. They used other tactics to torment her as well; only when her parents would arrive later in the day would she would have any sense of comfort.

One afternoon Nora found herself alone, crying and hugging her Shirley Temple doll, excluded from a party her cousins were having, when she sensed that someone else was in the room with her. "Opening my eyes, I saw an old Chinese man standing just inside the closed door. He was smiling at me, and he looked older than anyone I had ever seen before. His kindly face was full of wrinkles, and the hair of his head and beard was very long and very white. He was wearing the clothing of a servant, a long blue overshirt that hung to the floor."

*How did he get in?* Nora wondered. Her door was closed. She had not seen or heard him enter; instead, he seemed to have materialized: "He was just suddenly there." She decided that he must be a new servant of her grandmother's. He then addressed her in Mandarin: "Don't be afraid, I come from God." Then, "as if he had been reading my mind," the old man said she should not cry because she had not been invited to her cousins' party. "But I'm so lonely," Nora blurted out. "I don't have anyone to talk to."

He then addressed her by her full Chinese name: "Sung Neng Yee, you have prayed to God, and He has heard your prayer. He has sent me to be your friend, to comfort you and help you." Nora felt a tremendous sense of relief at the thought that she had someone to talk to, but she was also concerned, so she said, "Promise you'll come whenever I call you?" He promised, and he kept that promise.

She told her mother about her protector, and her mother asked to meet the old man, but Nora knew that was not possible. "Although I was the only one who ever saw him, the old man was helpful to us all," she wrote. "He came to see me almost every afternoon, and he would tell me such useful things as the best time to get in line for the rice ration for our family." One day the old man brought her important news. He told her that she would leave the house and her tormentors, and would travel from Shanghai to a distant city to meet her grandfather. Her grandfather was in Chungking, China's wartime capital, an area the Japanese did not occupy. When the girl told her parents this news, they demanded to learn more. They asked her to summon the old man, and she did, but again, he only appeared when she was alone. He said they would leave in one week.

They did leave a week later, on a harrowing weeks-long journey. Nora and her parents were dressed as beggars, in filthy clothes. They smeared dirt on their faces and carried little of value. They traveled first to Nanking, avoiding Japanese soldiers along the way. Their faces were burned in the sun. Walking wore down their shoes. They headed out beyond the city onto rugged paths. They stopped for the night, about ten miles from the border of the zone of the Japanese occupation, and they huddled together to sleep in a deserted shack but were awoken by men who burst in and demanded they give up what little they had. After the terrifying experience they decided to keep walking. But as they approached the border, they saw Japanese soldiers pacing back and forth, guarding it.

They did not know how they could possibly get past them. "Many in the group—including my parents—felt that death was a certainty. We had spent thirty-seven days of living hell walking and running, suffering hunger and thirst—all for nothing," Nora recalled. In the dead of night they made the crossing, and as they approached the line they got down onto all fours and crawled before finally standing and running the last few yards. Nora had prayed for help and believed that God or her angel had intervened. Safely in Chungking, in her grandfather's luxurious home, bathed and fed, Nora no longer felt lonely or in danger. "I didn't even need the old man," she wrote, and the angel was gone.

**DEREK RODRIGUES WAS IN DALLAS** to attend an aunt's funeral. He was traveling early in the morning, around 6 A.M., in February, when the driver of his car nearly lost control of the car on an icy bridge deck. Derek urged her to pull over, to wait until the sun had time to warm the road, but she continued driving. On the next overpass she did lose control, and the car crashed into a telephone pole. Derek was thrown forward, and his head struck the windshield hard enough to crack the glass. After sitting stunned for a short time, he opened his door and stepped out of the vehicle, holding his forehead with his right hand. He walked to the front of the car to assess the damage and then returned to the passenger side, bending down to look at the damage to the front passenger-side wheel and axle. At that very moment his friend screamed his name.

Derek bolted upright and turned, only to see headlights racing toward him. Another car had been sent out of control because of the ice, and that vehicle struck him. He was literally sent flying, upward and backward through the air for many yards. It only lasted a few moments, but Derek registered that he was moving higher and farther from the accident scene. He registered his friend's mouth open in horror. He thought he was going to die, but also felt that he couldn't possibly die. He was only twenty-one—too young—and he knew that his death would in a sense mean two deaths, as it would also take his mother's will to live. Then, he saw his life flash before his eyes, beautiful scenes scrolling by in rapid succession.

He turned a little to the right to see where he was going to land hard. It was an automatic response. His brain was likely doing what it could to mitigate a very bad situation before he consciously could figure out any plan of action whatsoever. He saw some trees, then his outstretched arm, "and as my eyes were scanning down my arm to my hand," he was stunned by the sense that "a woman was holding my hand and wrist, guiding me into the only possible thing that I could hit, and survive."

Derek could feel the tangible presence of an angel on his right side. He had no doubt that she was an angel. He felt her close to him, and a sense of peace filled him. In fact, he said, "it was probably the calmest and most comforting point I've ever reached." As Derek put it: "I was fine with my fate, because of her."

He was thrown against one of the support cables for the telephone pole, and he hit the cable at precisely the right angle and in the right place in order to survive. His back struck the cable so that it ran directly up the middle of his back but slightly to one side so that there was no damage to his spine. "If I had hit the cable below my waist," he said, "I would have flipped backwards; if it was higher towards my neck, I would probably be paralyzed; if I had totally missed the cable, then I would have landed in the woods behind that or, worse, would have hit the telephone pole directly."[11]

The impact had the effect of a slingshot, sending him backward toward the vehicles, and he landed in the ditch at the side of the highway. Remarkably, the car hit him just below the knees, making Derek think that he must have jumped, instinctively, just before the impact. As a result, his knees were fine, and the only injuries that he sustained were whiplash and multiple fractured ribs on the right side of his back where he hit the support cable.

This had all only taken a matter of seconds, and yet everything had slowed to a crawl for him. The driver of the car that hit him was still sitting behind the wheel, as if in shock. But when he got up, the driver, a nurse, helped get him to a hospital. "She thought that she had killed me. She couldn't believe that I was alive." Remarkably, Derek looks back on it now as a wonderful experience, one that he would not give up or alter if it were to happen all over again.

CLAUDE THORMALEN, a twenty-year-old in the US Army's 82nd Airborne Division, was making combat-type training jumps from a C-130 on a drop zone out of Fort Bragg, North Carolina. The early morning sky was full of military aircraft and paratroopers jumping out of them, and when Claude looked out, the air below seemed to be full of parachutes.

The average weight of a paratrooper was about 165 pounds, and at the time Claude was six-foot-four and weighed around 200 pounds. As a result he always fell faster than everyone else around. This time, on exiting the plane at twelve hundred feet, his parachute opened normally, but he quickly saw that there were several men just below him and he was catching up fast. He shouted that he was going to slip his chute to the right and they should slip to the left. He came down hard on his riser, spilling a great deal of air out of his chute, and saw that he was about to land on one of the other men's chutes. As he came down on the other chute he lost all the air out of his own parachute and it collapsed. Thormalen shot past the man, and his main chute began to spiral above him. He immediately went into a jump position with his back straight and his legs parallel to the ground, and he popped his reserve chute and tossed it to the side. He looked up and saw the reserve go directly into his main. They both began to tangle and spiral. Claude's first thought was, "I am dead."[12]

He then immediately felt a presence near him and behind him. He also felt very calm. And, despite apparently plunging to what seemed would certainly be his death, he felt no fear at all. It all happened very quickly, but then a powerful, commanding voice said, "Do what you were trained to do!" At that point Claude estimated that he was about six hundred feet from the ground and falling fast. But he did what he was told to do. He very calmly began to attempt to pull his reserve chute back out of his main and redeploy it. "I was not having any luck, as they were both tangled badly and not helping at all in slowing my fall, but I kept trying. Throughout this whole experience I was very calm and without a trace of fear or apprehension."

Still, the reserve must have caught some air, and when he hit the ground he was knocked unconscious but was not killed. He believes he was only out for a short time, because when he regained consciousness there were only a couple of men standing over him, and they had not even checked for vital signs. "As I came to, I felt very good and was not the least surprised I was still alive. I got on my feet and took care of my chutes, gathered my gear, and continued on with my assigned mission." The presence, which had been with Claude for those terrifying minutes, was gone.

IN SEPTEMBER 2008 Stephanie Neilson was traveling in a light plane on a day trip over the Arizona desert. Her husband, Christian, had recently qualified as a pilot, and alongside his instructor, they were flying to New Mexico and back. It was on the return jaunt that the plane crashed and exploded. The instructor was killed, her husband injured. For Stephanie, what followed was a terrifying scramble to survive. She gave a riveting account of her battle in her book, *Heaven Is Here*.

Stephanie was on fire and was moments from death when "someone arrived to help me. I knew it was my grandmother, but not by sight. I just knew."[13] The presence actually guided her hand as she unfastened her seatbelt, "then she led my hand to the handle of the airplane door, and together we opened it." Stephanie was able to get out of the wreckage, and her grandmother immediately told her to "roll" in order to put out the flames. Stephanie did as she was instructed.

Stephanie had burns over 80 percent of her body. She was in critical condition when she reached the hospital, and for the next three months she was in a medically induced coma while doctors treated her burns. When she emerged from the coma she began to try to reconstruct events, to understand what had happened. "Scattered images flashed through my mind. A wall of orange flames. The pungent smell of burning skin mixed with jet fuel." She remembered the help she had received from a seemingly impossible source. "I heard a voice telling me to roll. I believe it was an angel," she said. "I felt the presence of my grandmother."[14] With that sudden intervention, and only seconds to react in a situation of sheer terror, Stephanie was able to survive the plane crash.

A TWELVE-YEAR-OLD New Jersey schoolboy, David Janssen was invited for a weekend sleepover at a friend's house, a split-level apartment, on the sixteenth story of a building overlooking the Hudson River. He had never been there before, but he liked his friend, Hunter, and it seemed like it would be fun.

That evening Hunter's father hosted a large party, and the apartment was crowded. David and his friend were the only children and were sort of bored as they listened to music and watched a film with a group of adults. It was kind of the typical "I am a kid hanging out at an adult party" type of evening.

As the night wore on, David and Hunter were sent off to bed, which was in a room on the lower level of the split-level apartment. They talked for a while and then, despite the din of the party, were soon asleep. David was awakened with a start a few hours later by screams, which continued for a few moments. It was early, around 6 A.M. He got up to investigate and realized there was smoke in the hallway. He followed a trail of smoke until he ran into a wall of fire on the upper level of the apartment. The entire area was engulfed in flames.

By then the screams had ended. He would later learn that Hunter's father had died in the blaze. There was now only the intense roar of the flames and bottles popping in the extreme heat. David ran back and shouted at his friend, who was a little younger, that the apartment was on fire. David did not tell him about the screams—too much was happening.

Hunter ran into the next bedroom to call the fire department. David didn't know what else to do. He didn't think about closing the bedroom door and putting wet towels down to keep the smoke out; he was twelve. There were no adults in the apartment, at least none alive. "It is odd, but I didn't see any real way out, and I felt it was too much of an inferno to really stop. I didn't expect the fire department to have ladders large enough to reach us."

It was terrifying—with the smell, the sounds, and the sense that there was absolutely no escape. Hunter was still talking to the fire department, and David returned to the bedroom he had slept in. It was then that things started to change. He wasn't upset or frantic; instead, a "strange peace" completely embraced him. "I was sitting on the bed, realizing there was no way out and it was here that I would die. I lay down on the bed, with my head on the pillow, looking at the ceiling. And then, it came. It was an overwhelming sense of peace and serenity. It kind of descended upon me. This is the only way I can describe it. I didn't think about my friend, or my family, or much of anything. Nothing was disturbing me. I guess that seems so odd."

While he was lying on the bed, after a minute or so, David heard the voice. "After experiencing the peace or tranquility, I had stopped really trying to figure things out or plan a strategy," he said. "The voice was just suddenly there, and was a stark interruption. It wasn't in my train of thinking and called me to a different set of instructions and thought. I wasn't thinking about strategy or defense; I was just coming to grips with the fact that this was the place I would die in. I had given up trying to figure it all out.

"Someone was there at that moment. It was not a woman's voice, but a man's voice. I am not sure I thought to myself, 'I feel someone else is in the room,' as things were happening so rapidly, but I knew someone was there, and he gave me the only way out. It was information I did not have. I would call it a presence."[15]

The voice was abrupt and had a sense of urgency. "It wasn't my kid voice; it was an adult voice." It gave strict orders: "Get up. Go over to the window. Look down."

"It was imperative," David recalled, "and it spoke in a command voice. I had confidence in the voice, as it brought an idea I had never contemplated. It was a voice of authority in the midst of utter destruction. I know that it was not my thought, as I had finished looking for an escape, and the thought of looking out any window never dawned on me. Frankly, what would be under that particular window but a parking lot sixteen floors below?"[16]

David immediately followed the instructions. He glanced over to where there was a window and got up and walked to it, craning his neck to look down. "To my utter amazement, balconies started two floors below! The voice was right! There was a way out."

He ran into the adjoining room to get Hunter, who was still on the phone with the fire department or someone. David shouted, "We can get out—follow me!" He was now in an entirely different state of mind: he was in survival mode. "I wasn't afraid. I was confident that we were going to get out. I was going to get us out. I really didn't have the time to talk about how I found this out; in fact, I never told him. I just wanted us out of there. And I now knew the way."

The two boys went back into the bedroom, and David opened the window and instructed Hunter to follow him. He crawled out and, facing back into the room, extended his arms and then dropped through the air before hitting the balcony on the fourteenth floor. He was in bare feet and hit hard, but he then rolled to the side because he knew Hunter would be following. They landed on a balcony of an empty apartment. They yelled for help and pounded on the glass. After a short time David saw a woman on the other side of the divider, so he crawled over the top to her side of the balcony. "I explained that there was a fire and we had jumped. I told my friend we would be right back with someone to get him off the balcony. The lady took me downstairs. By this time the fire department had come, and I was given to a fire-man or a policeman." Hunter was rescued soon after.

David didn't tell anyone about the presence at the time; he just didn't know how to explain it. "I just wanted to be a normal kid that was concerned about when the Mets were playing again and when I could go to the beach," he explained. He didn't mention it until he told a girlfriend, later his wife, when he was eighteen and in college. Later he told his children and a few close friends. It was too personal to share more widely. He has never heard the voice or felt a presence again, though he has never faced a life-or-death situation again either.

"I think to myself, what if nothing had been under that window? But, it doesn't seem to happen that way. There is a way out, and the way of the passionate voice is correct." From the moment of his escape to this day, David has never thought that the presence and its voice were a product of his brain. He was not raised in a religious household; he had no preconditioning in the sense that he cannot recall the subject of God even being mentioned while he was growing up. Yet he felt at the time and to this day that it was a spiritual experience. "I knew I was somehow not alone in the room, though I could not tell you where the presence was localized. It just existed."[17]

After what had happened, he had a strong desire to attend church, told his mother that, and soon began attending an Episcopalian church. He eventually entered the ministry. David says that his brush with death and hearing the voice of a calming presence altered the course of his life. "In a very real way it was the experience by which all other experiences are understood," he said. "It was as if for a moment in time a celestial curtain was briefly raised and lowered again. The glimpse of the mystery is, for me, the most precious knowl-edge I have in life."[18]

David has considered the various scientific theories for the sensed presence as well as auditory hallucinations, and though he doesn't dispute the research, nor does he think it disproves the spiritual basis of his own experience. "I am not at all bothered by the search for localities in the brain that, under the right medical-induced stimulus, may mimic the presence," he explained. To the contrary, he argued that it may even provide proof for it.

He says that if God or an angel were to communicate with people during moments of great stress and trial, those mes-sages would still be received and interpreted through the brain's cognitive systems and information processes. "Would not the messages sent from the divine actually stimulate brain activity? I expect they would. Why wouldn't they? The question for me is not whether the brain is stimulated but the source of the message," he said.

Research, like that undertaken by the Swiss neurologists working with an epileptic patient, has not settled that ques-tion. Were the words spoken to him with such clarity and ur-gency—"Get up. Go over to the window. Look down"—and the vivid physical presence that he felt in the room at that moment really the product of what he terms, "the closed sys-tem of a brain with a world view that is only material?" How could the brain steer him out of danger with information it could not have had? And even if it had done so, why would the brain leave the impression that it was the product of the supernatural world and "coat the process with a sense of in-ternal foreknowledge, omniscience, internal direction, and a predestination of outcomes"?

David Janssen has carefully studied the evidence and has not been moved from his conviction, stating, "Whether scientists can stimulate a brain in similar ways does not, for me, conflict with a supernatural being we call God or angels who may indeed be able to enter the human experience at critical moments to show the path out."

MIKE AQUILINA SUGGESTED that there are things we each can do to "get the most from" our guardian angels. It's important to remember, for example, that our guardian angel is always watching us, watching how we treat others, how we parent, if we are kind to small animals, how we behave morally, and so on. As he puts it: "We tend to behave better when we know someone's watching."[19]

Our own guardian angels are not the only things we need to think about, he said. Children have guardian angels too, so in a typical nuclear family of four, there are four divine beings watching and potentially available to help. Then there are the angels assigned to other family members, friends, and coworkers. They are also there to help as long as it is also in common with their ward's interest. So it's possible to leverage considerable angelic assistance, if required.

Fundamentally people need to be conscious of the presence of guardian angels, said Aquilina, and "get in the habit of calling upon them for little favors." Not only can they help with mundane things like finding a good parking spot, but he believes people should ask them to keep them healthy and safe, even if they are under no obligation to do so. "Go ahead and call upon your angel every time you start your car or cross a busy street," he urged. The very process of thinking of angels, he said, is a good thing if "our natural desire for safety brings heavenly assistance ever to our minds."

This is one way to attempt to elicit the Angel Effect, but I suspect it is not the only one and likely not the most effective either. Can this capacity be evoked intentionally? Can angels be summoned? Direct paths to the presence have been used for millennia.

# - 9 -

# EVAGRIUS

# THE

# SOLITARY

## PRAYER AND MORTIFICATION OF THE FLESH

**EVAGRIUS PONTICUS HAD A PROMISING ECCLESIASTI-**
cal career in Constantinople. By AD 380 he had risen
to the rank of archdeacon and had developed a name for
himself beyond church circles. According to Palladius: "He
flourished in the great city, speaking with youthful zeal
against every heresy" while at the same time living a "luxurious and refined and voluptuous life." He was "handsome in
person, and careful in his mode of attire."

Along the way Evagrius became infatuated with a married
noblewoman, and the attraction was mutual. The woman
"was pressing and madly excited," but Evagrius, fearing God
and ashamed by his strong feelings and temptation to sin,
wanted to end the flirtation. He was under great duress, in
part for fear that he had provoked "the jealousy of her husband, who plotted his death." Evagrius felt powerless because of her superior rank, so he prayed fervently for some
obstacle to be thrown in the path of the looming affair.

His prayers were answered by "an angel vision in the
shape of soldiers of the governor, and they seized him and
took him apparently to the tribunal and threw him into the
so-called custody, the men who had come to him, as it
seemed, without giving a reason having first fastened his
neck and hands with iron collars and chains. But he knew in
his conscience that for the sake of the above fault he was
suffering these things, and imagined that her husband had
intervened." This "saving vision" understandably had a great
impact on Evagrius, who became extremely anxious. In the
vision others were being tortured, and he was chained alongside forty prisoners, so he was given a taste of the unhappy
fate that awaited him if he persisted.

The angel then intervened again, this time having transformed into the form of a sympathetic friend who asked, "Why are you retained here, my lord deacon?" Evagrius replied, "In truth I do not know, but I have a suspicion that so-and-so the ex-governor has laid a charge against me, impelled by an absurd jealousy. And I fear that the judge corrupted by bribes may inflict punishment on me."

The angel made him swear that, in exchange for freedom, he would leave Constantinople and care for his soul. Evagrius took the vow, saying he would leave by ship, "Except for one day, to give me time to put my clothes on board, I certainly will not remain." With that the chains fell off his wrists and the vision ended. He did as he had pledged: he placed his possessions on a ship and sailed to Jerusalem.

Old habits are hard to shake, however, and, as his disciple Palladius wrote, with "vain-glory stupefying him," Evagrius soon fell back on his previous ways. His efforts to live a monastic life were undone in part because of his concern for his appearance, in particular a love of clothes, which he changed often. He was, however, punished for this, afflicted by a bout of fever that was followed by a terrible illness that persisted for six months, "drying up his flesh, the source of his trouble." Physicians were summoned and were powerless to heal him, but a saint intervened. He confessed everything, and she said to him: "Give me your word before the Lord that you will keep to the mark of the monastic life; and, sinner though I am, I will pray that you may be granted a furlough of life." And he consented.

In AD 383 Evagrius arrived in Nitria, a monastic community in Egypt near Alexandria, and after that he moved on to

Kellia, a remote desert community, where he embarked on an ascetic life of penitence. He fasted, eating barley gruel or porridge once a day. He restricted even the amount of water he drank. He stopped bathing. He cut his sleep to only four hours a day. He also engaged in prolonged standing to inhibit his passions, As Palladius put it: "The demon of fornication troubled him grievously, as indeed he told us himself. And all night long he stood naked in the well, so that his flesh was frozen." Continued Palladius: "On another occasion again the spirit of blasphemy troubled him. And for forty days he did not enter under a roof, as he told us himself, so that his body threw out ticks."

Described as "the first architect of Christian spiritual discipline," Evagrius's intense interest was in the problem of the "disturbing thoughts" that plagued him, each of which he associated with a demon.[1] Essentially, he saw demons as a "way of expressing the unwilled nature of certain mental events." He classified the demons, producing a treatise on the "Eight Spirits of Wickedness," which listed them, in order, as gluttony, fornication, avarice, anger, sadness, aecia (sloth/dejection), vainglory, and pride. This list influenced what would later become the Seven Deadly Sins.

In a recent study Jonathan Hill argued that Evagrius, because of his obsessions with "thoughts, impulses or images," as well as other factors, may have had obsessive-compulsive disorder. "At very least he had many of the traits that are associated with the disorder," Hill wrote in the *Journal of Medical Biography*, adding that he "could well have had the symptoms sufficiently clearly to be diagnosed with OCD were he alive today."[2]

To overcome the disturbing thoughts, Evagrius adopted a succession of mental and physical practices aimed at restricting sensory stimulation in order to achieve "a cognitive grasp of the simple presence of God." He sought to "deprive himself of all mental representations" and perfect detachment from the senses in order to "commune with the one who is beyond all representations and sense perception."

The desert was the foundation of his practice: "The desert was a place of restricted environmental and social stimulation and a religious symbol of freedom from established society. It was a spiritual terrain with geographic features."[3] On top of the geography and climate Evagrius built layer upon layer of austerities: dispassion and prayer; fasting; dehydration; sleep deprivation in the form of all-night vigils, some involving endurance standing; religious weeping; prostrations; exposure to extreme heat and cold; mortification of the flesh; and self-administered blows to the chest and face.

He was not alone in adopting a severe regimen and engaging in self-punishment, however. An army of ascetics populated the desert. Estimates vary, but there were at least five thousand of them. The extremity they sought and reached is hard for us to comprehend. Evagrius wrote of one monk who stood "under a rock for three years in uninterrupted prayer, not sitting at all or lying down, but simply snatching some sleep while standing." Another, Symeon Stylites, remained on a pillar for years, virtually motionless. Even a seeping ulcer on his foot was not enough to get him off his perch.

The ascetical theologian John Climacus, abbot of St. Catherine's monastery, wrote, "From the number of their prostrations, their knees seemed to have become wooden, their eyes dim and sunk deep within their sockets. They had no hair. Their cheeks were bruised and burnt by the scalding of hot tears. Their faces were pale and wasted. They were quite indistinguishable from corpses. Their breasts were livid from blows; and from their frequent beating of the chest, they spat blood."

As they approached death, other monks would gather around, asking whether "the door has opened to you, or are you still under judgment?" or "Have you felt any enlightenment in your heart, or is it still dark and ashamed?" They were seeking some sign of a light at the end of the tunnel. It didn't always come, but there were many occasions when it did. In his study, "Brain and Psyche in Early Christian Asceticism," David T. Bradford wrote, "Such practices reshape the mental state, including toward mystical experience."[4]

The ascetical goal was in part to attain a status much like an angel: "Angels are depicted as asexual creatures untroubled by the desires and gravity imposed by physical form," wrote Bradford. Not only did they seek to transcend bodily desires and necessities; "the ascetic sought to become angelic by miming the angels' loving intentions and approximating in prayer their contemplation of God."

If not outright angelic, at very least their practices could bring them into the company of angels. In one instance a sixth-century ascetic engaged in repetitive prostration, completing a grueling regimen of eighteen hundred, in sets of one hundred, during daily visits to a cave-like pilgrimage site. After ten years of this, upon completing his final prostration, he "envisioned two angelic figures surrounded with lights." This was the fulfillment of this one monk's long journey. Such experiences were the goal of the devotion and, ultimately, the suffering. As Bradford wrote, "the feeling of presence has broad application in the study of religious experience. Angels, souls, and saints might appear as spatial presences."[5]

THE PRACTICE OF SEEKING PRESENCES is as old as humanity. It was there at the birth of Christianity, and until very recently, tribal cultures around the world practiced it. Some found that rhythmic drumming could summon spirits. This phenomenon is described in the Arctic, where "Ecstasies developed after intense drum-beating and the substitution of ear-splitting shouts for songs.... In this ecstatic state, the shaman would begin to hallucinate, as though he could see [natural surroundings] where his spirits were to be found."[6] The shaman would then share the messages the spirits communicated to him with the expectant audience.

Indeed, practices for invoking a sensed presence exist in many cultures around the world, from the Shamanic traditions of the Plains Indians to the ancient Greeks, from Christian mystics to Indian yogis and Western occult practitioners. With all these traditions, people have set out deliberately to invoke the company of an unseen presence. It is actually possible to "train the human mind to experience the supernatural."[7] This capacity can be evoked intentionally, and, as the desert monks discovered, angels can be summoned.

The spirit quest bears much in common with the aesthetic practices of the desert monks. Marking a rite of passage from childhood to adulthood for North American Indians, it has been characterized as a "sought vision induced by hunger, thirst, purgatives, and self-laceration." Young men would be sent away and, with time—alone, hungry, frightened, physically debilitated—"he may be visited by what, he thinks, are supernatural beings." Among the very earliest written reports of a spirit quest was one recorded by a Jesuit missionary in 1642. In it a young man, "when but fifteen or sixteen years of age, retired to the woods to prepare himself by fasting for the appearance of some Demon." After living in isolation and in a state of near-starvation for sixteen days, "he saw an aged man of rare beauty who came down from the Sky, approached him, and looking kindly at him said: 'Have courage. I will take care of thy life.'"

A famous example involves Crazy Horse, the Lakota warrior who led five hundred braves to defeat Major-General George Armstrong Custer at the Battle of the Little Bighorn. Crazy Horse had a vision, likely in 1860–1861, which gave him the strength and confidence to fight for his people, a people who were herded into crowded reservations, who suffered disease and were made to give up their traditional way of life.

Crazy Horse followed the usual practice—going for days without food or water, alone—when he experienced a spiritual presence. He looked at a blade of long grass, which, when he studied it closely, revealed a path down to a small lake. He followed the path into the water and then "A man on horseback came out of the lake and talked with him." The being gave Crazy Horse advice, which he adhered to throughout his life, telling him not to wear a war bonnet, not to paint his face as was the practice of Lakota warriors, but to instead rub dirt from a gopher hole on himself and to wear straws of grass in his hair. The being also "told him he would never be killed by a bullet, but his death would come by being held and stabbed; as he actually was." This was oddly comforting to Crazy Horse, who emerged from the experience renewed and strengthened. At age twenty, he found the encounter with the "man from the lake" had transformed him into his people's most fierce warrior.

Lakota elder John Fire described the impact of such experiences, saying the vision "is not a dream; it is very real. It hits you sharp and clear like an electric shock. ... You are wide awake and, suddenly, there is a person standing next to you who you know can't be there at all ... yet you are not dreaming; your eyes are open."[8]

THE SENSED PRESENCE is something more, then, than a spontaneous phenomenon that arrives in times of stress and danger; it is something that can be provoked. The desert monks discovered that deprivation and extremity could allow them access to such experiences, but the real path was found not in the austerities—the fasting, prolonged standing, and prostrations. Instead, it came in the form of a simple prayer that involved the "cognitive grasp of the divine presence."

To Evagrius, experience with the presence is not the product of careful analysis or great learning, nor can it be "probed and plumbed as if it had 'parts' that might become clear and meaningful."[9] On the contrary, he sought to move beyond all mental representations, to detach from senses in order to "commune with the one who is beyond all representations and sense perception."

This form of contemplative prayer, first practiced by Evagrius and others in the desert of Egypt some seventeen hundred years ago, holds the key to something extraordinary. Today, people are not likely to emulate the desert monks through self-flagellation and such, and they probably won't embark on a spirit quest with its similar physical and psychological toll. But if there is another way to evoke a sensed presence, a simpler way—a prayer—then all bets are off. If you accept the teachings of Evagrius, we are perhaps looking at a fundamental human capacity, a trainable skill.

Bradford gathered Evagrius's writings on his approach to the prayer:

(1) Do not by any means strive to fashion some image or visualize some form at the time of prayer.

(2) Blessed is the mind which during the time of prayer has acquired perfect detachment from the senses.

(3) Strive to render your mind deaf and dumb at the time of prayer and then you will be able to pray.

(4) The mind possesses vigour when it imagines nothing of the things of this world during the time of prayer.

(5) Prayer is a state of the mind destructive of every earthly mental representation.

These ideas were also propagated in the fourth-century writing of another notable desert father and a disciple of Evagrius's, St. John Cassian. A monk from Southern Gaul, Cassian was the first to introduce the rules of Eastern monasticism to the West. He wrote of an "ardent prayer which is known and tried by but very few, and which to speak more truly is ineffable; which transcends all human thoughts." Aspects of that practice can be found in many important mystical works, from *The Cloud of Unknowing* to the rapturous prose of St. Terese of Avila and St. John of the Cross. It nearly was forgotten, however, as "Knowledge of how to practice contemplation in Christianity has ebbed and flowed over the centuries and became nearly lost in the modern and postmodern eras."[10]

In fact, there *is* a current Christian practice, called the centering prayer, which people use deliberately to invoke the company of an unseen presence. It is a form of prayer that can be traced directly to Evagrius and the desert fathers. As David Frenette, a leader of the centering prayer movement and author of *The Path of Centering Prayer*, explained to me: "The Christian contemplative tradition affirms that God's presence can be experienced interiorly at increasingly subtle levels. Language falls short in trying to describe the experience of God, but it can include felt sensation in the body (like warmth, pleasure, lightness), feelings (such as love and joy), auditory or visual perceptions (of messages, light, images of God), the mind (the silencing of thought—the peace that passes all understanding) and effects in consciousness (like the radiance of pure awareness without any perception or thought)."[11]

This particular form of contemplative prayer emerged during the early 1970s in order to offset the movement of young Catholics toward Eastern meditative techniques. Promulgated through the teachings of the Trappist monks Thomas Keating, William Meninger, and M. Basil Pennington, all of whom were influential American Roman Catholic mystics and thinkers, the centering prayer is said to allow ordinary people to "experience God's presence ... closer than consciousness itself."

The practice requires an individual to focus attention on a phrase from the Bible and, by its internal repetition, not only invite what practitioners feel is the presence of God but also to elicit perceptional changes, such as "loss of the usual sense of space."[12] A study of Franciscan nuns performing the centering prayer demonstrated that the practice was associated with increased cerebral blood flow in the frontal lobes as well as the superior parietal lobe, which is associated with spatial perception.

Subsequent studies have expanded on this finding, suggesting that "long-term meditators have different activity patterns in their brain compared to non-meditators." One study argued that "meditation might induce such changes in brain activity over a period of time. In either case, the implication is that different patterns of baseline brain function are associated with different religious and spiritual practices." Practices like the centering prayer "affect beliefs and experiences through a fronto-parietal network since these structures have consistently been involved in both the acute practice of meditation and, now, in the long-term effects of such practices. In addition, the frontal lobes have been suggested as an important mediator in the sense of self and altered states of consciousness."[13]

In 1974 Father Meninger, then living at St. Josephs Abbey in Spencer, Massachusetts, discovered "a dusty little book in the abbey library." Entitled *The Cloud of Unknowing*, the book is an anonymously written spiritual guide from the Middle Ages that presents contemplative meditation as a teachable, spiritual process. It was originally written in Middle English, not in Latin, and so was obviously written for laymen, not priests or monks.

Within a year of its rediscovery *The Cloud of Unknowing* had given rise to the first workshop teaching the centering prayer; eventually a company was established to assist in teaching the practice, and tens of thousands have since mastered the technique. Moreover, Father Meninger's own book, *The Loving Search for God*, has sold over a million copies. What is intriguing about all of this is that it is the contemporary manifestation of a practice that has been cultivated since antiquity. The "angel effect" lies at the very root of mystical traditions—in both the East and the West—with a secret history that runs like an underground current from ancient times through to modernity.

Using this method of prayer, people have set out deliberately to invoke an unseen presence. When they do so, very specific things happen, for the experiences share a common, reproducible phenomenology. The practice takes time, but its cumulative effects cannot be overstated.

Frenette has an evocative way to describe it. "God's presence," he said, "is like the cinema screen upon which all of a film's images are projected. At the movies, we normally are quite caught up in its drama and not aware of the screen. At the end of the movie, if we stay long enough, we will finally see the screen that was there all along."[14] The centering prayer allows people to see that screen; indeed, such a presence can become a full-time companion in a practitioner's life. They are never alone. They can become like Yana Jovnyruk.

**DRIVING HER NISSAN ULTIMA** from her home just outside of Toronto, Yana was headed to Guelph, Ontario, where she was taking flying lessons. It was early one evening in November 2005, and it had started to snow heavily. Yana, twenty years old and an inexperienced driver, did not ease off the pedal. She had her music cranked up and was traveling too fast for the conditions. Her car began to slide, and Yana was unable to regain control of the vehicle, which skidded off Highway 6 and then began to flip. It rolled three times before landing on its roof. Through those terrifying moments and for some minutes after the car came to a rest, a presence took control and calmed Yana.

During the accident the loud music seemed to stop—at least she wasn't hearing anything or doesn't remember hearing anything. "It was like someone changed the radio channel," she recalled. "In place of the music was an authoritative voice. It told me exactly what I needed to do. It was comforting. It told me to keep breathing; it told me my life was not over. I just kept receiving these instructions." It was more than the reassuring voice, however. There was a presence. She felt warmth on her right hand, as if it were being held or grasped. This began as the car slipped off the highway and began rolling and continued after it stopped, as she hung upside down, still strapped in with her seat belt. Somehow the sensation of a hand was also a comfort to her.

After a few minutes—she felt it could have been as long as ten minutes—other drivers arrived to help her. At the moment when they arrived, the voice fell silent and Yana's sense of a presence ended. "People came to help me; they pulled me out of the car, which exploded a short time later."[15] Her rescuers were examining her, trying to determine how seriously she had been injured. "They were looking for signs of trauma and could not believe it, because there weren't any. Only a bruise on my left shoulder where the seat belt had been." This was later confirmed in the hospital, where she was taken by ambulance. There was no concussion. She was not even very shaken up emotionally. She was basically fine. One of the people who aided her said, "Someone was definitely watching over you."

That person didn't know the half of it.

Yana is different from many of the people in this book in one important way. She learned at a very young age that unseen companions protected her, and her sense of having a guardian angel has been with her ever since. As a child of six living near Ivano-Frankivsk in western Ukraine, she would hear voices giving her directions. This happened, for example, if she got off the bus at the wrong stop; the presence would guide her to the correct stop and then to her home. "Knowing I had an angel with me, I never felt alone. I was always being guided and protected." One accompanied her when she went to school: "I sensed that he was an older man." The feeling that someone was with her never frightened Yana; on the contrary, she understood immediately that "their purpose is for you to have a life with less stress and more happiness. They are there to guide you through it." She moved to Canada with her family when she was thirteen years old, and she had a sense that her angels accompanied her.

When she was eighteen years old she was dating a man who was seven years older than her. He was taking steroids, and the drugs seemed to affect his moods. He could be easily set off and would fly into a rage. Sometimes these would turn violent. One night they went out to a bar in downtown Toronto. Over the course of the evening the man became very aggressive. Initially his anger was directed at her, but soon other people intervened on her behalf and were drawn into what became a melee. Someone called the police, and the man was detained.

The officers asked Yana what had happened and whether she wanted to press charges. Her instincts were to protect her boyfriend, but just as she was about to speak and downplay the incident, an angel interceded. "You have to tell the truth. Then this will be over," a voice said to her. She surrendered to the advice, remembering, "I did what I was told. I didn't make excuses." It was the right decision. It ended a destructive relationship that, if she had persisted in it, would have resulted in a very different life. Yana said that some people refuse to acknowledge the voices or the sense of a presence but that, for her part, "After that day, I knew I would always have to follow them. It's important that you trust them. Sometimes it is your last resort."

She keeps coming back to that word: trust. She said that so many lives would be so much happier if people could accept that they have a friend with them. "People live with this capacity but they cannot acknowledge it," she said. In many cases, people need to be "hit hard" before they wake up to this potential. Said Yana: "Sometimes we ignore the little signs we get. Sometimes extreme situations have to happen in order for us to acknowledge this reality."

Yana has some advice. "You cannot analyze it," she said. "If you do, your logical brain will discard it. You will seek to rationalize what is happening, you will try to understand it as a scientific occurrence. But it doesn't work that way. You simply need to trust it, at that moment. There is a purpose behind it, and it can transform your life." She advises people to start by opening themselves up to a "few little nudges each day, and follow the guidance they receive." It requires practice to permit these hints and directions. In Yana's words: "it's like going to the gym."

She also said that meditative techniques like the centering prayer can assist people to experience a presence. "People who are multitaskers in their daily lives—and many people are—would have a hard time with this one because their brain would have trouble staying in the moment and putting itself on mute. In order to experience a presence, people need to shut down their brain temporarily. The amazing thing about practices like the centering prayer is that if done on a regular basis, it can act like a scheduled appointment with your guardian angels, where you show your intention to seek their guidance, and they are absolutely ready to help."[16]

# - 10 -

# RJ

## AND THE

# LAWNMOWER

# ANGEL

## CONCLUSION

WRITING THIS BOOK HAS BEEN A PROFOUND LEARNING experience for me. It has brought me to a place I never thought I'd get to. Looking for explanations, I found something else instead: I found humility, and I found meaning.

Looking at the accounts of sensed presences across cultures and across situations, what became abundantly clear is how common the experience is. Although in the secular West we most often experience this angelic other in times of great stress, for so many others—children, devotional folks, people in other cultures, and some exceptional people like Yana—the sense of being connected to some externalized caring presence is utterly commonplace. It is a regular part of their lives, whatever they choose to call it—and many call it an angel or God. Far from being pathological, when you look at the actual metrics of these special peoples' lives—at their subjective descriptions of happiness and fulfillment, at their rates of sickness and mortality—what emerges is a sense of extreme mental health. I have already outlined some of these benefits, but this book is focused on just one: this sense of companionship strengthens their lives immeasurably.

To show you how it can work, consider Shawn Allaire. Shawn has struggled with what she calls "aloneness" much of her life. An only child born of an alcohol-wrecked marriage, she feels that a ribbon of loneliness has been woven through her journey. She says that this "has always been a mystery to me." It is not a situation of her choosing. Shawn likes people and has been married twice, yet she has spent a great deal of time alone. Even today she feels she is in a situation of "extreme solitude" despite living amongst the 122,000 inhabitants of Thunder Bay, Ontario, her hometown.

In 1990 Shawn had already experienced a major heartache with the end of a relationship, and soon after she was involved in an automobile accident that left her badly shaken. Her sole surviving parent, her father, then fell seriously ill, and she traveled to Winnipeg to be near him. "I remember how grief would wash over me. There was nothing I could do but cry. At that point I was so drained by life, I had no defenses left. I remember that vividly. I could not do the thing we all do: keep up a face, hide our feelings so we don't disturb others. I did not have the strength for that. I was so alone and so sad, with no defenses that the presence 'got in.' Thankfully. It gave me strength to go on."[1]

She was walking along a busy street in Winnipeg as her father lay dying in a nearby hospital. "Somehow, in the midst of the pain, there came an awareness of something comforting behind my right shoulder keeping pace with me ... just there, and comforting somehow. It did not intervene at all. There was exactly that feeling of being surrounded by warmth and caring as one might have when your mother is nearby, caring and loving. There was no communication, just a feeling of not being alone in grief."[2] Since that time she has come to a startling realization: "I have the ability to access the sensed presence on a daily basis if I need to."

Shawn derives great strength from this incredible gift or capacity to summon this "benevolent being" at critical times, when her sense of isolation seems acute. "I don't abuse it. I realize that this is something special, something to be cherished," she said. "I don't want to lose the ability to access it, and so I approach it with respect, yet I always know the presence is there, in the background, and will be there for me if I truly need help, not only in an emergency but just comfort in a desperate moment of loneliness."

This awareness profoundly altered Shawn's life for the good; it has lifted her out of her sense of social isolation. "I find the experience of being alone is in the process of changing for me. It loses some of its prickliness now that I can allow another, even an incorporeal other, to be close to me. And that this being is benevolent and compassionate provides the comfort that sometimes the outer world seems to lack."

So the presence does not come only to those in imminent physical danger, nor is it always restricted to one intervention. For Shawn, as with some others who have contacted me, the presence had become an ongoing part of her life.

Consider the implications of this. Research shows that one in ten people report feeling lonely "often." That is a staggering figure. In 2008 a major study of loneliness outlined three factors that determine how lonely people feel, based on, first, their level of vulnerability to social disconnection; second, their ability to self-regulate the emotions associated with feeling isolated, and finally, the danger that people who feel lonely are likely to exaggerate the extent to which they are seeking companionship and, hence, are further harmed by a perceived failure to have it reciprocated.[3] Each of these factors varies widely from person to person, and they are determined by a set of precipitating conditions, including genetic. What if, however, that one person in ten could find a way to do what Shawn Allaire did? What if we could generate our own companionship or acknowledge the companionship that exists? There would be no reason to be alone ever again.

Of course the question we must ask as good secular investigators is whether or not this presence is "real." Certainly it is real as an experience. It is far too common and has been described by far too many people to be anything but that. However, is the sensed presence also an actual autonomous entity out in the world? Or is it the product of some private neurobiological upwelling, as is the scientific opinion?

The skeptics are right to critique the looseness of many angel reports, to recognize their catchall nature; as one skeptic put it: "Literally any experience could be an angel-experience." Although this may be the case, it is too limited an explanation, not far from the "demon-haunted world" that Carl Sagan famously warned us of, in which anyone can believe anything. Science here has been a liberation—to shed light on the deeper mechanisms underlying our experience, mechanisms that exist independently of what we might wish them to be. This is part of what was so thrilling for me when researching this book. While investigating the various social and biological scientists with their multitude of theories, I found that there is something galvanizing and empowering about this. Science is exciting, but it can also fall short. It makes sense to me that scientific research could stimulate the feeling of a presence while not being able to replicate the love or benevolence of the experience as so many describe. Physiological, biochemical, and electrical measurements are only correlates to consciousness and intentionality and meaning. The mind cannot be reduced to the brain.

What causes the sensed presence? There are so many theories and so little agreement. Although I admire the research and am excited by the direction the science is taking, after a while the sheer number of competing explanations began to take on a comic feel, as together they demonstrate that no one quite knows what is happening here. The very same critique the skeptic levels toward angel aficionados can also be directed toward neurologists and cognitive psychologists. Any experience can be a brain-induced experience. There is always another mechanism to unveil, another recombined cognitive process or two (or three) that can be hypothesized.

In this game sometimes it seems as though the well-meaning and enthusiastic scientist can propose just about anything and then build them into a reassuring story, one that is usually based, not coincidentally, in their particular niche area of expertise. This is a version of what psychologists call "confirmation bias," when aspects of some case that supports one's ideas are highlighted and other inconvenient aspects ignored or explained away. Certainly when it comes to the full "angel effect" experience—the sensed presence, the exact helpful advice, the sometimes paranormal physical intervention, the relaying of circumstantial information the subject couldn't possibly know—not one of these reductive theories can explain them all in their totality.

The problem with the neurological theories is that they fail even to acknowledge the fundamental property of the sensed presence, namely that a majority of people feel a benevolent being of great power has touched them, so they assign it a spiritual identity. For Kevin Gillen, it was God; Jane Pottle, Durwin Keg, and many others also felt it had some sort of spiritual basis. Bishop Alexis Bilindabagabo felt angels protected his mission. Derek Rodrigues not only felt it was an angel, but he also saw one. John Robbins is less certain but doesn't dismiss the possibility that it was a guardian angel. Joe Losinski feels it could have been God but is also not sure.

In my own case I have a conviction that it was my son, but I also felt as if the presence were something greater than my son. In my circumstance, I do not need to take a great leap of faith to consider the possibility that I had a spiritual experience, that I sensed an angel. The only theory that really seems to explain it is Thomas Aquinas's divine intervention, but that will certainly not satisfy this book's secular readers.

What is interesting is that no matter their individual explanations regarding the basis of their experiences, not a single one of the people whose cases I have mentioned failed to acknowledge the unusual nature of what they had encountered. They are not people who have gone about their lives looking for evidence of God's good works. Many, in fact did not or do not practice religion. And they are aware that some people will question their stories and that, of those people, some will attribute what happened to a stress-induced mind pushed to the breaking point. They are also aware that others will be still less generous and will say that they made it all up. And yet they are unmoved and stand by their belief that it was, in most cases, a spiritual encounter.

THESE PEOPLE ARE NOT ODDBALLS or crystal-ball gazers. They are people like you or me, except that they have been in conditions of extreme stress and, as a result, experienced something that has, in some cases, saved their lives and, in others, changed their lives. Ask yourself: How is it that Susan Morris, a fourteen-year-old girl being sexually assaulted in a crack house, a terrified child being threatened with a gun, could travel through that horror and arrive at a place in which she can now say it transformed her life and that she would never exchange it to return to the life she had before or the person she was before?

And Susan is not alone.

In his best-selling *Heaven Is for Real*, Todd Burpo told of a report from his three-year-old son, Colton, after surviving a close call—an emergency appendectomy—"that he had spoken with angels." It seems an astonishing claim to make. Here is a child, innocent to the ways of the world, offering a testimonial to the existence of the spiritual realm. But in the context of the hundreds of cases that have flooded in to me from people who say they have been visited by angels, or at least benevolent presences that walk and talk like angels, Colton's report is hardly astonishing at all.

Take the case of another three-year-old, RJ, who was on a riding lawnmower with his father when he was bounced off and run over. It was October 1993, and RJ was sitting on top of the mower when, in an instant, he fell. His mother, Alice, was inside the house when she heard two horrific screams. "I went running to the door to find my husband hollering for me to call 911 and carrying my bloody son to me."[4] Miraculously, the boy survived, but he had very serious injuries. His right arm was hanging by the skin, he had a great deal of his skull exposed, his back had been sliced open by the blades, showing the ribs and lung on one side. He was also cut on the face, with a gash from his mouth to his ear. Alice felt he was very nearly killed: a little deeper, and his scalp would have been cut to the brain, or if the injury on his back was located just a few inches differently, his spinal cord could have been severed.

Alice rode in the ambulance with RJ, and despite the serious injuries, he didn't cry the entire way, except briefly when the paramedics started an IV on him, "Stop that! You're hurting me," said the small red-headed boy. He was rushed immediately into surgery. After he received medical attention, he and his mom were in the hospital room when she realized that RJ had seemed at peace during this ordeal. Later, when he came to after the operation, his mother asked him why he had not cried or seem scared. He looked at her and replied, "Momma, I wasn't scared because the angels wrapped their wings around me." He then added matter of factly: "It sure was windy under there."

Later that year while shopping, Alice found a Christmas ornament with an angel holding a little red-headed boy. She said the family still hangs it on the Christmas tree every year, "to thank the angels and God for their blessing of life."

Or take the case of Mary Jane Goddard.

In the early evening of Friday, August 13, 2010, a "huge bang" destroyed a large yellow farmhouse in Sussex Corner, New Brunswick. People miles away felt the powerful blast. MJ was inside the home, sitting on the sofa with her dog, Mickey, when she quite literally "went up with the house."[4] She recalls feeling "like a rag doll (shot) from a cannon."

MJ is uncertain how high she was thrown, but when she reached that height, her body bent in half and then she began to fall. Her hair was standing on end as she plummeted back into the ruins of the house. This was probably a reflection of the speed she was dropping, and yet she experienced an entirely different sensation. MJ felt as if she was drifting back to earth, "back and forth", like an autumn leaf. It was as if she was riding on a "magic carpet," she said.[5]

MJ's husband, James Harvey Goddard, was killed instantly by the explosion, the cause of which remains unknown. As for his wife, her survival was nothing short of miraculous.

The house had been levelled, but even her impact into the debris was not what she expected. MJ does not remember how she landed but suspects it was on her feet. "I did not feel panic or fear at all. My focus was on finding Mickey. I remember putting my hand up to my face and feeling the warmth running over it: I knew I was bleeding. I looked to my left and there was darkness, I looked to my right and again darkness. When I looked directly in front of me I saw lathe, it was a wall with the plaster missing off of it."[6]

MJ began to choke from the dust and smoke when "all of a sudden I felt a strong presence surround me. I was in some kind of protected zone." This vivid presence then spoke in what she says was a strong male voice: "You have to think clearly now." She felt somehow safe. Then a light revealed a path out of the debris. It was as if she was being led out from the danger. "I knew I had to go to that light, in my mind I was thinking 'that is the Light or that is the sunshine: either way I have to go to it.'" As for the voice, she has no doubt as to its origin: "I knew the only voice that I heard was that of God's voice."

WE HAVE LOOKED THROUGH the various neuropsychological theories, but there is another possibility. The simplest explanation is that the sensation of a benevolent presence is veridical, that it is what it seemed to these people to be. It certainly fits with what we are taught to expect. By tradition, one of the first things an angel says is, "Fear not."

That is not to say that some of the scientific research does not need to be taken seriously, however—the work of the neurobiologist Olaf Blanke, in particular. When activating an electrode in a patient's brain—between the parietal and temporal cortex—Blanke immediately induced the feeling of a sensed presence, "as if turning on and off a light switch." This would seem to prove the physical origins of this sensation. There is an "angel switch" in the brain. End of story.

Except even here the phenomenon may not be so easily explained away. It doesn't explain the paranormal stuff, for one. Jane Pottle and Yana Jovnyruk, for example, each described feeling a hand holding theirs. Others describe an invisible barrier that protected them from injury. But we also have to look carefully at what this study is really telling us: that it is possible to induce this sensation on demand doesn't mean there may not also be times when the sensation is an actual perception. We can induce auditory hallucinations on demand, but this doesn't mean real sound doesn't also exist. Sometimes it may be a delusion; other times it may be a real perception. It needn't be an either-or case.

But there is an even deeper critique here that has to do with the nature of consciousness itself. In the West most of us live inside the materialist assumption that the brain creates the mind. This may be true, or it may be false. We don't understand the relationship between mind and matter. It is a mystery—perhaps our most profound mystery. William James, the great father of modern psychology, made no such assumptions. In a famous lecture on the brain he argued that we cannot know whether the brain is like a producer or a transmitter. Does the brain produce the mind, like a lamp produces light? Or is it more like a prism or a lens, refracting a preexisting phenomenon into the full spectrum of our personality? The answer to this question will be very different depending on what you believe about the relationship between the mind and the brain. And make no mistake about it: where you land on this particular question is an article of faith, however scientific your world outlook may be. For his part, James preferred the transmitter model. In other words, this eminently rational pioneering psychologist had strong mystical sympathies, which the many brain scientists who reify James often downplay.

So is the brain triggering a sensed presence? Yes, perhaps so. Or it may simply be revealing a presence that is already there. The angel switch in the brain may be more like one of English writer Aldous Huxley's "doors of perception."

I sought a definitive explanation but came to realize the truth is that the answer presently does not exist. Maybe some newly discovered mechanical cause will address all the features of the angel experience; although, to be honest, given so many of the impossibly paranormal details, I don't know how it could. But it might. Or we might find that there are dimensions of experience that exist outside our current material accounts of reality. This too is possible, and it could happen within a perfectly naturalistic universe—after all, there will be a twenty-second-century science as sure as there is a twenty-first-century one, and its discoveries are sure to be as surprising to us now as our own science would no doubt appear to nineteenth-century investigators.

If we are genuinely open-minded, then we must be humble, as most scientists are humble in the face of the universe's staggering complexity. This is true skepticism. Certainly in my own case I felt more and more humility as I researched this book; that is, I began with a search for an explanation, but the more explanations I found, the more humility I found. I began to accept that I am okay with not knowing. This, finally, is our right, one that no one can take from us. The scientist has the same right: to choose the explanation that satisfies him.

I know what I experienced that night. I was visited by a presence that was every bit as real as having a flesh-and-blood person in the room with me, only more so in the sense that it had a strong sense of emotionally immediacy. I felt comforted and, in a tangible way, better. I am not a religious person, so when I set out to find an explanation for what happened, I expected to find it among the numerous studies I delved into. Yet none of the theories I investigated seemed quite right.

I set out to find an explanation and instead came to question the need to find explanations. I began to champion uncertainty and subjective meaning over objective explanation. I suddenly found myself confronting the reactive materialist need to explain everything away, to find "the answer."

The fact is that *we don't know* what's behind these episodes. The sheer number of competing explanations proves this. We don't know enough about how the mind meets the world to make any definitive conclusions. There is a better path, however, and it is to sit courageously inside this kind of agnosticism, to rest in the unknown without contracting around some final "answer." This seems to me the mark of true intellectual and spiritual maturity.

My experience with my son, James, forced me to go further than what I found in the research literature. Because although it may be true that at the moment we can't know what is ontologically true, we can know what has value and meaning in our lives.

When I looked at that tiny, outwardly perfect boy and watched all the promise that he represented drain away, I lost more than a baby; I experienced a loss of faith of sorts. I felt my prayers had not been answered. But I realize now that my faith was restored when James returned. If I have lost any faith now, it is in the likelihood of a satisfying scientific explanation of that visit as well as for all of the cases outlined in this book.

Many of the psychologists who look at grief and mourning and the phenomenon of a sensed presence after death have changed the way they think about the issue. Studies show these experiences are deeply reassuring and comforting, providing positive benefits. In fact, they may be a very healthy response to the loss. To have these experiences explained away—especially when there is no decisive brain case to be made—is to do a disservice to these people's experiences—to my experience.

If it's true that the only *sensible* conclusion is agnosticism, then for me, ultimately, the only *practical* conclusion—that is, the only conclusion that will actually improve my life and health—is faith in the possibility and the potential of the unknowable. The knowledge that James is still out here in some way, the experienced fact of his presence, makes my life immeasurably richer and more meaningful.

This is my right, and it is yours, just as it is the right of others to choose an overactivated temporal lobe as their preferred explanation. They are not cosmically correct—we don't know what's really true. This is simply their own preferred article of faith. The scientist's proof is a reproducible effect delivered via an electrode. Mine is an experience that changed my life.

So I have landed in a paradox, torn between my agnosticism around explanations on the one hand, and, on the other, my growing certainty that James was with me that night. F. Scott Fitzgerald has a famous quote: "The test of a first rate intelligence is the ability to hold two opposed ideas in the mind at the same time, and still retain the ability to function." I don't pretend to be a first-rate intelligence, but I find this reassuring. I feel as though there is wisdom in being able to live inside a paradox, and I am not alone.

Explanation and meaning live on two very different dimensions of knowing. One will never satisfy nor replace the other. It's rather like trying to replace a trombone player in an orchestra with a can of red paint. They are different art forms. Maturity, for me, is learning to live with a paradox, that although I may never know the real explanation for James's reappearance in my life, I can nevertheless live with the truth that he is still real for me, just as all of the sensed presences in this book are real for the people who experience them. They are, quite literally, a mystery we can live with.

I have been visited by an angel, if you'd like to call it that, in the form of the presence of my dead son. He did what angels do: he offered me hope, he comforted me, and he guided me during a time of despair. The sensed presence is the most compelling experience that any of us is likely to encounter in our lives. Think of it: we are lonely, we are under stress, we are threatened, so we reach out to find a friend, a helper, a benevolent being. But are they Heaven-sent, or are they the products of the human brain, or are they both? I think I know what the answer is.

# NOTES

## INTRODUCTION: JAMES

1. Peter Suedfeld and John Geiger, "The Sensed Presence as a Coping Resource in Extreme Environments," in *Miracles: God, Science, and Psychology in the Paranormal*, vol. 3, J. Harold Ellens, ed. (Westport, CT: Praeger, 2008).

2. Ron DiFrancesco, interview with author, August 23, 2005.

3. Steven Schwartz, MD, Death Summary, James Sutherland Angus Geiger, July 5, 2007.

4. A. M. Stiggelbout, A. C. Molewijk, et al., "Ideals of Patient Autonomy in Clinical Decision Making: A Study on the Development of a Scale to Assess Patients' and Physicians' Views," *Journal of Medical Ethics* 30, no. 3 (June 2004): 268–274.

5. Ibid.

## CHAPTER 1: THE TUCSON NUN

1. Jane Pottle, e-mail to author, July 20, 2012.

2. Ruth Montgomery, *Threshold to Tomorrow* (New York: Fawcett Crest, 1988), 148–149.

3. Ibid., 148.

4. Jane Pottle, e-mail to author, July 31, 2012.

5. Ibid.

6. Robert A. Hummer, Richard G. Rogers, Charles B. Nam, and Christopher G Ellison, "Religious Involvement and U.S. Adult Mortality," *Demography* 36, no. 2 (May 1999): 273–285.

7. J. M. Wallace Jr. and T. A. Forman, "Religion's Role in Promoting Health and Reducing Risk among American Youth," *Health Education and Behavior* 25, no. 6 (December 1998): 721–741.

8. T. Seeman, L. F. Dubin, and M. Seeman, "Religiosity/Spirituality and Health: Psychological, Behavioral, and Biological Determinants," *American Psychologist* 58 (2003): 53–63.

9. Kiri Walsh, Michael King, Louise Jones, Adrian Tookman, and Robert Blizard, "Spiritual Beliefs May Affect Outcome of Bereavement: Prospective Study," 324, no. 7353 *British Medical Journal* (June 29, 2002): 1551–1553.

10. Jennifer Agiesta, "AP-GfK Poll: Nearly 8 in 10 Believe in Angels," *Guardian*, December 23, 2011, www.guardian.co.uk/world/feedarticle/10008985.

11. Scott Draper and Joseph O. Baker, "Angelic Belief as American Folk Religion," *Sociological Forum* 26, no. 3 (September 2011): 623–643.

12. David Van Biema, "Guardian Angels Are Here, Say Most Americans," *Time,* September 18, 2008, www.time.com/time/nation/article/0,8599,1842179,00.html.

13. Draper and Baker, "Angelic Belief as American Folk Religion."

14. Susan Morris, correspondence with author, April 7, 2012.

15. Arthur Agnew, interview with author, April 3, 2013.

16. Ibid.

17. Some of these thoughts were inspired by Gary Williams's excellent review of *The Third Man Factor*: "Book Review: John Geiger's The Third Man Factor: Surviving the Impossible," September 9, 2012, Minds and Brains, http://philosophyandpsychology.wordpress.com/2012/09/09/book-review-john-geigers-the-third-man-factor-surviving-the-impossible/.

18. Emily Stimpson, "The Mysterious Third Man," Our Sunday Visitor, November 15, 2009, www.osv.com/tabid/7621/itemid/5587/The-mysterious-Third-Man.aspx.

19. Elizaveta Solomonova, Elena Frantova, and Tore Nielsen,

"Felt Presence: The Uncanny Encounters with the Numinous Other," *AI and Society* 26, no. 2 (May 2011): 179–186.

20. Ibid.

21. J. A. Cheyne, "The Ominous Numinous: Sensed Presence and 'Other' Hallucinations," *Journal of Consciousness Studies* 8, no. 5/7 (2001): 133–150.

22. James Allan Cheyne, "Sensed Presences in Extreme Contexts," Skeptic, April 22, 2009, www.skeptic.com/eskeptic/09-04-22/.

### CHAPTER 2: THE RWANDAN BISHOP AND THE BROOKLYN RABBI

1. Bishop Alexis Bilindabagabo, with Alan Nichols, *Rescued by Angels: The Story of Miracles during the Rwandan Genocide* (Brunswick East, Australia: Acorn Press, 2001).

2. Bishop Alexis Bilindabagabo, e-mail to author, December 8, 2012.

3. Ibid.

4. Yoram Bilu, "'We Want to See Our King': Apparitions in Messianic Habad," *Ethos* 41, no. 1 (2013): 98–126.

5. Ibid.

6. Michal Kravel-Tovi and Yoram Bilu, "The Work of the Present: Constructing Messianic Temporality in the Wake of Failed Prophesy among Chabad Hasidim," *American Ethnologist* 35, no. 1 (February 2008): 64–80.

7. Bilu, "'We Want to See our King.'"

8. Ibid.

9. Ibid.

10. Elizaveta Solomonova, Elena Frantova, and Tore Nielsen, "Felt Presence: The Uncanny Encounters with the Numinous Other," *AI and Society* 26, no. 2 (May 2011): 179–186.

11. Ibid.

12. Yorum Bilu and Gabriel Herman, "Visions and Apparitions from an Interdisciplinary Perspective," workshop synopsis.

13. Bilu, "'We Want to See Our King.'"

14. Translation of a recorded interview, available at: http://video.yehudim.net/play.php?vid=1392http://video.yehudim.net/play.php?vid=1392 (translation by Amir Gavriely).

15. Kobi Nahshoni, "Rabbi Yosef Describes Rachel's 'Manifestation' in Gaza," ynet news, Jewish World, January 25, 2009, www.ynetnews.com/articles/0,7340,L-3661283,00.html.

16. Gabriel Herman, "The Third Man Factor/Sensed Presence as Historical Fact," paper presented at Visions and Apparitions from an Interdisciplinary Perspective, Jerusalem, May 2013.

17. Kobi Nahshoni, "Rabbi Eliyahu: I Sent Mother Rachel to Gaza," ynet news, Jewish World, January 21, 2009, www.ynetnews.com/articles/0,7340,L-3659308,00.html.

18. Herman, "The Third Man Factor."

19. Gabriel Herman, "Greek Epiphanies and the Sensed Presence," *Historia: Journal of Ancient History* 60, no. 2 (May 2011): 127–57.

20. Graham Wheeler, "Battlefield Epiphanies in Ancient Greece: A Survey," *Digressus* 4 (2004): 1–14.

21. 2 Macc, 3.24–25.

22. 2 Macc. 3.27–28.

23. Herman, "The Third Man Factor."

24. Edwards Gibbon, *The Decline and Fall of the Roman Empire*, vol. 2. (New York: Modern Library, 1932), 293.

25. Kent G. Hare, "Apparitions and War in Anglo-Saxon England," in *The Circle of War in the Middle Ages*, Donald J. Kagay and L. J. Villalon, eds. (Woodbridge: Boydell Press, 1999).

26. William A. Christian Jr., *Apparitions in Late Medieval and Renaissance Spain* (Princeton, NJ: Princeton University Press, 1981), ch. 2. http://libro.uca.edu/christian/apparitions2.htm.

27. Ibid.

28. William A. Christian Jr., Visionaries: The Spanish Republic and the Reign of Christ (Berkeley: University of California Press, 1996). http://ark.cdlib.org/ark:/13030/ft5q2nb3sn/.

29. Francis Fernandez-Carvajal, *In Conversation with God: Meditations for Each Day of the Year*, vol. 7 (London: Scepter, 2005).

30. W. H. Prescott, *History of the Conquest of Mexico and History of the Conquest of Peru* (New York: Modern Library, 1936), 433.

31. E. Ann Matter, "Apparitions of the Virgin Mary in the Late Twentieth Century: Apocalyptic, Representation, Politics," *Religion* 31, no. 2 (2001): 125–153.

32. Michael P. Carroll, *The Cult of the Virgin Mary: Psychological Origins* (Princeton, NJ: Princeton University Press, 1986).

33. L'Osservatore Romano, July 11, 2001.

34. Matter, "Apparitions of the Virgin Mary."

35. "Former FBI Employee 'Saw Angels Guarding Flight 93 Site after Deadly Crash on 9/11'," *Daily Mail*, July 3, 2012, /www.daily mail.co.uk/news/article-2168337/Lillie-Leonardi-Former-FBI-employee-saw-angels-guarding-Flight-93-site-deadly-crash-9-11.html.

## CHAPTER 3: THE MEXICAN CLEANING LADY

1. Joseph Losinski, e-mail to author, January 14, 2013.

2. Joseph Losinski, "My Own Experience," www.thirdman factor.com.

3. David J. Roelfs, Eran Shor, Rachel Kalish, and Tamar Yogev, "The Rising Relative Risk of Mortality for Singles: Meta-Analysis and Meta-Regression," *American Journal of Epidemiology* 174(4) (August 15, 2011): 379–389.

4. Elizaveta Solomonova, Elena Frantova, and Tore Nielsen, "Felt Presence: The Uncanny Encounters with the Numinous Other," *AI and Society* 26, no. 2 (May 2011): 179–186.

5. Julian Jaynes, "Consciousness and the Voice of the Mind," *Canadian Psychology*, April 1986.

6. Helene Bass, "The Development of an Adult's Imaginary Companion," *Psychoanalytic Review* 70, no. 4 (Winter 1983): 519–533.

7. "Is It OK for an Adult to Have an Imaginary Friend?" discussion forum, http://forums.psychcentral.com/other-mental-health-discussion/147082-ok-adult-have-imaginary-friend-2.html.

8. E. Steffen and A. Coyle, "Sense of Presence Experienced in Bereavement and Their Relationship in Mental Health: A Critical Examination of a Continuing Controversy," in *Mental Health and Anomalous Experience*, C. Murry, ed., 33–56 (Hauppauge, NY: Nova Science Publishers, 2012).

9. Craig M. Klugman, "Dead Men Talking: Evidence of Post Death Contact and Continuing Bonds," *OMEGA* 53, no. 3 (September 2006): 249–262.

10. John Geiger, *The Third Man Factor: Surviving the Impossible* (New York: Weinstein, 2009).

11. Steffen and Coyle, "Sense of Presence Experienced."

12. Ibid.

13. Ibid.

14. Klugman, "Dead Men Talking."

### CHAPTER 4: THE TAPLOW PEASANT

1. Justin L. Barrett and Jonathan A. Lanman, "The Science of Religious Beliefs," *Religion* 38, no. 2 (2008): 109–124.

2. Jodie Swales, e-mail to author, May 2, 2013.

3. Jodie Swales, "You're Safe: An Angel's Got Your Back," *Christian Science Sentinel*, January 31, 2005.

4. Jodie Swales, e-mail to author, March 4, 2013.

5. Jodie Swales, e-mail to author, May 2, 2013.

6. James Allan Cheyne, "Sensed Presences," in *Hallucinations: Research and Practice*, J. D. Blom and I. E. C. Sommer, eds. (New York: Springer, 2011).

7. Tore Nielsen, "Felt Presence: Paranoid Delusion or Hallucinatory Social Imagery?" *Consciousness and Cognition* 16, no. 4 (December 2007): 975–983.

8. James Allan Cheyne, "Sensed Presences in Extreme Contexts," *Skeptic,* April 22, 2009, www.skeptic.com/eskeptic/09-04 -22/.

9. Cheyne, "Sensed Presences," in Blom and Sommer.

10. James Allan Cheyne and Todd. A. Girard, "The Nature and Varieties of Felt Presence Experiences: A Reply to Nielsen," *Consciousness and Cognition* 16, no. 4 (December 2007): 984–991.

11. Cheyne, "Sensed Presences in Extreme Contexts."

## CHAPTER 5: THE INTERPRETER

1. Peter Suedfeld and John Geiger, "The Sensed Presence as a Coping Resource in Extreme Environments," in *Miracles: God, Science, and Psychology in the Paranormal*, Vol. 3, J. Harold Ellens, ed. (Westport, CT: Praeger, 2008).

2. Todd Murphy, "The Sensed Presence and Vectorial Hemisphericity," www.shaktitechnology.com/sp.htm.

3. Matthew Roser and Michael S. Gazzaniga, "Automatic Brains—Interpretive Minds," *Current Directions in Psychological Science* 13, no. 2 (April 2004): 56–59.

4. Michael S. Gazzaniga, *The Mind's Past* (Berkeley: University of California Press, 2000).

5. Michael Shermer, *The Believing Brain: From Ghosts and Gods to Politics and Conspiracies—How We Construct Beliefs and Reinforce Them as Truths* (New York: Times Books, 2011).

6. Ibid.

7. Susan Denis, e-mail to author, May 3, 2013.

8. Susan Denis, interview with author, April 2, 2013.

9. Angele Blais Mackey, e-mail to author, May 8, 2013.

10. Julian Jaynes, *The Origin of Consciousness in the Breakdown of the Bicameral Mind* (Boston: Houghton Mifflin, 1976).

11. Suedfeld and Geiger, "The Sensed Presence as a Coping Resource."

12. Jaynes, *The Origin of Consciousness*.

13. Suedfeld and Geiger, "The Sensed Presence as a Coping Resource."

## CHAPTER 6: TOBY THE SWIMMER

1. Jeff Wise, "How Panic Doomed Air France Flight 447," *Huffington Post,* December 8, 2011, www.huffingtonpost.com/jeff-wise/how-panic-doomed-an-airli_b_1135004.html.

2. Ibid.

3. Michael Shermer, *The Believing Brain: From Ghosts and Gods to Politics and Conspiracies—How We Construct Beliefs and Reinforce Them as Truths* (New York: Times Books, 2011).

4. Michael Shermer, "The Sensed-Presence Effect," *Scientific American,* April 6, 2010.

5. John Geiger, *The Third Man Factor: Surviving the Impossible* (New York: Weinstein, 2009).

6. "The Flying Tiger Line Inc., Lockheed 1049H, N 6923C, Ditching in the North Atlantic, September 23, 1962," Civil Aeronautics Board Aircraft Accident Report, September 13, 1963.

7. "Richard and Lois Elander: 'A Fond Farewell,'" Flying Tiger 923, January 24, 2012, http://flyingtiger923.com/2012/01/24/major-and-mrs-richard-erlander/.

8. "Fred Caruso: Thank God I'm Alive!" Flying Tiger 923, July 26, 2012, http://flyingtiger923.com/2012/07/26/thank-god-im-alive/.

9. "Rachael: Hoopii: Hawaiian Mother, Daughters Vanish into Raging Sea," Flying Tiger 923, January 18, 2012, http://flyingtiger923.com/2012/01/18/mother-daughters-vanish/#more-315.

10. "The Flying Tiger Line Inc."

11. "Art Gilbreth: Out of Body Experience Guides Trooper," Flying Tiger 923, February 19, 2012, http://flyingtiger923.com/2012/02/19/out-of-body-experience-guides-trooper/.

12. "Fred Caruso: Thank God I'm Alive!"

13. Stephanie Heinatz, "Scarred Yet Strong Vet Stirs Wounded Troops," *Daily Press,* December 24, 2006, http://articles.dailypress .com/2006–12–24/news/0612240009_1_ryan-s-son-war-wounds -west-point.

14. Sandra McElwaine, "Pronounced Dead in Vietnam, Lt. Bill Haneke Inspires Post-9/11 Veterans," *Daily Beast,* November 11, 2012, www.thedailybeast.com/articles/2012/11/11/pronounced-dead -in-vietnam-lt-bill-haneke-inspires-post-9–11-veterans.html.

15. Rick Atkinson, *The Long Gray Line* (Boston: Houghton Mifflin, 1989), 336.

16. McElwaine, "Pronounced Dead in Vietnam."

17. Richard Webber, "It Happened to Me: My Guardian Angel Saved My Life," *Daily Mail,* December 4, 2009, http://www.daily mail.co.uk/femail/article-1233189/It-happened-My-guardian-angel -saved-life.html.

18. Ibid.

19. Ibid.

## CHAPTER 7: THE BALD WELDER

1. John Robbins, e-mail to author, January 28, 2013.

2. Jim Peacock, field notes, January 27, 1984.

3. Jim Peacock, e-mail to author, August 22, 2012.

4. Reed Branson, "Elvis Likeness Won't Be Part of Rose Bowl Parade," *Deseret News,* July 28, 1989, http://www.deseretnews.com/ article/57368/ELVIS-LIKENESS-WONT-BE-PART-OF-ROSE -BOWL-PARADE.html.

5. Pat Frascogna, e-mail to author, February 6, 2012

6. James Allan Cheyne, "Sensed Presences," in *Hallucinations: Research and Practice,* J. D. Blom and I. E. C. Sommer, eds. (New York: Springer, 2011).

7. "Explorer: The Angel Effect," *National Geographic Television,* 2011.

8. Kevin Gillen, e-mail to author, October 5, 2012.

9. Kevin Gillen, e-mail to author, October 8, 2012

10. E. Ann Witherspoon, e-mail to author, September 23, 2009.


CHAPTER 8: ROSA PARKS'S TWIN

1. Phil Taylor, "My Very Own Guardian Angel," *Pittsburgh Catholic,* March 2010.

2. Phil Taylor, "Color Barriers Don't Fall Easy, But They Fall," *Pittsburgh Catholic,* November 3, 1995.

3. Macdonald Critchley, "The Idea of a Presence," *Acta Psychiatrica Neurologica* 30, no. 1–2 (1955): 155–168. Reproduced in Critchley, *The Divine Banquet of the Brain and Other Essays* (New York: Raven Press, 1979).

4. John Geiger, *The Third Man Factor: Surviving the Impossible* (New York: Weinstein, 2009).

5. Scott Draper and Joseph O. Baker, "Angelic Belief as American Folk Religion," *Sociological Forum* 26, no. 3 (September 2011): 623–643.

6. Robert T. Carroll, "Angel," *The Skeptics Dictionary,* http://skepdic.com/angels.html.

7. Emily Bauman, "Dreaming in Crisis: Angels and the Allegorical Imagination in Post-War America," D-Scholarship @ Pitt, University of Pittsburgh, 2003, http://d-scholarship.pitt.edu/10404/.

8. Nancy Gibbs, "Angels Among Us," *Time,* December 27, 1993.

9. Mike Aquilina, *Angels of God: The Bible, the Church and the Heavenly Hosts* (Cincinnati, OH: Servant Books, 2009).

10. Nora Lam with Irene Burk Harrell, *China Cry: The Nora Lam Story* (Waco, TX: Word Books, 1980).

11. Derek Rodrigues, e-mail to author, September 4, 2012.

12. Claude Thormalen, e-mail to author, August 4, 2012.

13. Stephanie Nielson, *Heaven Is Here* (New York: Hyperion, 2012).

14. "Guardian Angel, Prayers, Family Help Woman Survive Horrific Plane Crash," MyNorthwest.com, June 3, 2012, http://mynorthwest.com/?sid=683554&nid=651.

15. David Janssen, e-mail to author, August 2, 2012

16. David Janssen, "In a Horrific Fire as a Child, This Is Why I'm Still Alive," The Third Man Factor, http://thirdmanfactor.igloo communities.com/forums/thirdmanexpersonalex/inahorrificfireasa childthisiswhyiamstillalive.

17. David Janssen, e-mail to author, March 1, 2013.

18. Ibid.

19. Aquilina, Angels of God.

## CHAPTER 9: EVAGRIUS THE SOLITARY

1. Jonathan Hill, "Did Evagrius Ponticus (AD 346–99) Have Obsessive-Compulsive Disorder?" *Journal of Medical Biography* 18, no. 1 (February 2010): 49–56.

2. Ibid.

3. David T. Bradford, "Brain and Psyche in Early Christian Asceticism," *Psychological Reports* 109, no. 2 (October 2011): 461–520.

4. Ibid.

5. Ibid.

6. Tassan S. Tien, Demitri B. Shimkin, and Sergei Kan, "Shamans of the Siberian Eskimos," *Arctic Anthropology* 31, no. 1 (1994): 117–127.

7. T. M. Luhrmann, "Hallucinations and Sensory Overrides," *Annual Review of Anthropology* 40 (2011): 71–85.

8. Lee Irwin, *The Dream Seekers: Native American Visionary Traditions of the Great Plains* (Norman: University of Oklahoma Press, 1994).

9. Bradford, "Brain and Psyche in Early Christian Asceticism."

10. David Frenette, *The Path of Centering Prayer: Deepening Your Experience of God* (Boulder, CO: Sounds True, 2012).

11. David Frenette, e-mail to author, March 12, 2013.

12. Andrew Newberg, Michael Pourdehnad, Abass Alavi, Eugene G. D'Aquili, "Cerebral Blood Flow during Meditative Prayer: Preliminary Findings and Methodological Issues," *Perceptual and Motor Skills* 97, no. 2 (October 2003): 625–630.

13. Andrew B. Newberg, Nancy Wintering, Mark R. Waldman, Daniel Amen, Dharma S. Khalsa, and Abass Alavi, "Cerebral Blood Flow Differences between Long-Term Meditators and Non-Meditators," *Consciousness and Cognition* 19, no. 4 (December 2010): 899–905.

14. Frenette, *The Path of Centering Prayer*.

15. Yana Jovnyruk, interview with author, June 1, 2013.

16. Yana Jovnyruk, e-mail to author, July 10, 2013.

**CHAPTER 10: RJ AND THE LAWNMOWER ANGEL**

1. Shawn Allaire, e-mail to author, December 6, 2012.

2. Shawn Allaire, e-mail to author, December 5, 2012.

3. John T. Cacioppo and William B. Patrick, *Loneliness: Human Nature and the Need for Social Connection* (New York: Norton and Co., 2008).

4. MJ Goddard, e-mail to author, January 25, 2013.

5. MJ (Parlee) Goddard, 'The House 1353', manuscript. Excerpt courtesy of MJ Goddard.

6. Ibid.

# INDEX

Absence of human contact, 62–65

Adamoli, Vida, and attack, 83–85, 90

Agnew, Arthur, and alcoholism, 13–16

Allaire, Shawn, and sensed presence, 201–203

Angel effect
description, 24, 120, 205
*See also* Sensed-presence phenomenon

Angels
Aquilina on, 19, 163–164, 178–179
Aquinas on, 159–160, 163
beliefs in, 8–9
children and, 207, 208
description/role, 7–8, 19–20, 24, 159–160, 196
skeptics on, 160–161, 204
*See also* Sensed-presence phenomenon

Angels, guardian angels
belief in, 9
concept history, 159
Critchley on, 158–159
description/role, 19–20, 159–160, 161, 163–164, 178–179
examples, 76–77, 157–158, 161–163, 164–178
*See also* Sensed-presence phenomenon

Angels in America (play), 163

Angels of God (Aquilina), 19, 163–164

Apparitions
ancient examples, 49–52
cultural stress and, 49, 51–52, 52, 53, 54
flood incident, 132–138
Israeli soldiers in Gaza, 39–43, 46
Schneerson and, 32–37, 39, 43, 46, 47, 54
temple riches example, 44–45
Virgin Mary, 47, 49–50, 52–54
*See also* Epiphanies; Messianic ecology

Aquilina, Mike, 19, 163–164, 178–179

Aquinas, Thomas, 159–160, 163, 206

Attila the Hun, 48

Aviner, Shlomo, 42

Azulay, Avner, 40–42, 43, 46

Bader, Christopher, 9

Baker, Joseph O., 9

Balej, Anthony, and loss/ depression, 66–71

Barrett, Justin, 85, 86

Baylor Survey of Religious Values and Behavior, 9

Beginnings of Rome, The (Cornell), 46–47

# ACKNOWLEDGMENTS

I would like to begin by thanking the people who contacted me and shared their own experiences. In many cases, what they lived through was very frightening and painful. It is not easy to talk about such things. I admire them for their courage and their conviction. Without their willingness to step forward and share these often deeply private experiences, *The Angel Effect* would not have been possible.

I would like to profoundly thank, in no particular order, Arthur Agnew, Susan Morris, Durwin Keg, David Janssen, Jane Pottle, Kevin Gillen, Bishop Alexis Bilindabagabo, Joe Losinski, Anthony Balej, Paula Riddle, Vida Adamoli, Claude Thormalen, Jodie Swales, Kelly Smith, Liz Gregori, Melissa Fox-Revett, Susan Denis, Carol White, Angele Blais, John Robbins, Jim Peacock, Pat Frascogna, Brian Lumley, Ann Witherspoon, Erich Brinkmeyer, Derek Rodrigues, Yana Jovnyruk, Shawn Allaire, Janice McCurry, RJ McCurry, and Suzie Boatright. They are just a few of the many people who I spoke to, and while some of the accounts shared with me do not appear in this book, they are no less compelling.

The body of scholarly research around the phenomenon of the sensed presence is growing, and I would like to acknowledge particularly the groundbreaking work of Professor Gabriel Herman and Professor Yorum Bilu. I would also like to thank a friend and past coauthor of mine, Dr. Peter Suedfeld.

I'm grateful for the advice and suggestions of Jeff Warren, a fine conceptual editor, thinker, and guru of sorts. For more on Jeff visit his website, www.jeffwarren.org. There are a few other people whose encouragement and friendship kept me on course these past few years, especially André Préfontaine. Thanks to Pat Mullins, a fantastic web guru, and Andrew Lovesey, who is the same to social media. Also, I will never forget Victor Spinetti and Leila Hadley Luce.

No book would have been possible without my agent, Patrick Walsh, and his compatriots at Conville & Walsh. I would like to also thank my editors, Jennifer Lambert at HarperCollins and Amanda Murray at Weinstein Books, as well as Christine Marra, for their patience and encouragement.

Most of all I want to thank all the members of my family, my parents, all four of them, Marina, my sons Alvaro and Sebastian, and of course James. I established a fund in his name, www.jamesgeigerfund.com.